*Tomorrow's Leaders*

# CHURCH AND CAMPUS

J. J. Murray

Francis Pickens Miller

R. T. L. Liston

John R. Cunningham

Ernest Trice Thompson

Malcolm C. McIver

René de Visme Williamson

D. Maurice Allan

Dallas H. Smith

Hunter B. Blakely

*edited by DeWitt C. Reddick*
*original drawings by Eleanor Shell*

# CHURCH
## AND
# CAMPUS

*Presbyterians Look to the Future*
*from Their Historic Role*
*in Christian Higher Education*

---

# JOHN KNOX PRESS
RICHMOND, VIRGINIA

Library of Congress Catalog Card Number: 55-12361

First printing, January, 1956

# *Foreword*

WE WHO are members of the Presbyterian Church in the United States need to be asking ourselves some searching questions about what we are doing in higher education.

Until the dawn of the twentieth century, the state left much of the task of higher education to church colleges and other private colleges. Until then, the church college provided education for many where otherwise education was not available. In the twentieth century, the state has risen to the challenge with large universities, teachers colleges, and specialized institutes. Has the day come when the church—or to be more specific, our own Presbyterian Church in the United States—is no longer needed in higher education? Could we make better use of the $715,273.46 contributed to church college budgets last year by applying it in other fields of service?

This leaves us facing the question in a realistic manner: What is a church college? In what way does it make such a distinctive contribution to the Christian nurture of youth that it justifies the support of the Church? A heavy burden is placed upon the trustees and the administrative staffs of church colleges to see that their institutions, while maintaining a challenging intellectual level, likewise discover means of undergirding their whole educational philosophy with more of an awareness of the will of God.

Likewise, we are confronted with the sheer numbers to be cared for in institutions of higher education. The generation now in our elementary grades will have twice as many individuals in college as did the generation of their parents. Will this human tide have to be regarded as the responsibility of the state? Or should church colleges double their enrollment, thus vastly increasing the cost to the Church?

As you will see, these problems are not simple. Neither are

5

other challenging questions: How can we best go about ministering to those thousands of Presbyterian students on the campuses of our state universities? And how can we develop the evangelistic zeal to reach the considerable proportion of students, on campuses of both church and state institutions, to whom religion has little vital meaning?

Those of us in the Church feel comfortably stirred when we hear one of our leaders say: "If we can capture for Christ the college generation of today, we will enlist tomorrow's leaders of the world." Literally, the statement is true. But it will remain only a glittering generality unless you and I, as individual members of the Presbyterian Church, discover some way to do something about it.

Neither can we neglect the increasing complexities of education for the ministry and for full-time Christian work. There was an age, not too long ago, when the minister could count on being one of the few educated persons in his community; and his opinions were likely to go unchallenged. Too, the minister was primarily a preacher and a pastor. Today, with the higher levels of education and the increased interrelations of all aspects of living, the minister finds it more and more difficult to be well informed. As churches grow, he must be a business manager and an executive; and he should have some understanding of personnel policy and principles of public relations. His counseling leads him into areas that require a knowledge of psychology and an understanding of emotional maladjustments. How can we make sure that the educational training of our ministers and full-time workers keeps abreast of changing needs?

Running like a dark shadow beneath all the challenges for educational progress is need of money. Education is expensive business. No matter how zealously the staff of a church college wants to admit all worthy young men and women, to do so will demand new classroom buildings, more teachers' salaries, more dormitories. Salaries are now much too low. And to reach college students at state institutions will require full-time paid leadership.

To ensure that worthy students can attend college when they lack personal financial resources, scholarship programs must be extended. A recent survey of a number of colleges revealed that the average assistance per student for the 1952-53 school year was $85.21.

Therefore we can say with Dr. Hunter Blakely, author of the last chapter of this book, "Now is the time for decision."

You may well say, "But these are problems for the leaders of the Church. Let them come up with some solutions."

Such a statement disposes of our responsibilities too quickly. The questions will not be answered in a Christian way without the understanding, the thinking, and the sharing of all who belong to the Presbyterian Church.

It is upon this premise that we invite you to read this book carefully. Its chapters have been written by men who have labored long in the field of Christian service to youth through education. The writers would be the first to acknowledge that though they see the problems, they have not perceived all the answers clearly. They need your help. The book may not be as easy to read as a popular novel or one of our mass magazines; but we can assure you that it will be more rewarding.

DeWitt C. Reddick
Austin, Texas

# Contents

1. *The Critical Years*
   STUDENTS FACE NEW FREEDOMS........................ 10
   *J. J. Murray*

2. *For Dignity of Man and Glory of God*
   PRESBYTERIAN COLLEGES AND HUMAN LIBERTY............ 28
   *Francis Pickens Miller*

3. *Blood, Sweat, and Prayers*
   HOW PRESBYTERIANS BUILT THEIR COLLEGES.............. 48
   *R. T. L. Liston*

4. *What Is a Christian College?*
   ITS CONTRIBUTION AND SIGNIFICANCE................... 70
   *John R. Cunningham*

5. *The Presbyterian Mark: An Educated Leadership*
   YOUR SEMINARIES AND TRAINING SCHOOL................ 88
   *Ernest Trice Thompson*

6. *Campus Christian Life*
   STUDENT RELIGIOUS WORK ON ALL CAMPUSES............. 112
   *Malcolm C. McIver*

7. *Called to Witness*
   FACULTY CHRISTIAN MOVEMENT....................... 126
   *René de Visme Williamson*

8. *Serving God Through Lifework*
   PRESBYTERIAN GUIDANCE PROGRAM.................... 144
   *D. Maurice Allan and Dallas H. Smith*

9. *A Time for Decision*
   PRESBYTERIANS LOOK TO THE FUTURE.................. 160
   *Hunter B. Blakely*

## CHAPTER 1

## JOSEPH JAMES MURRAY

Pastor, Lexington, Va., 1924—.

Attended Davidson College, Union Theological Seminary, Free Church College of Glasgow, Scotland, and Oxford University in England.

Chairman, Board of Christian Education, Presbyterian Church in the United States, 1949-55, and member of Board for many years.

Long-time worker with students and faculties of Washington and Lee University and Virginia Military Institute.

Author of four books and co-author of three others.

Authority on bird life and at one time the only Southerner on the executive committee of the National Audubon Society.

# The Critical Years

## STUDENTS FACE NEW FREEDOMS

## *by J. J. Murray*

IT WAS the early autumn of 1954. The Advisory Council on Higher Education was in session on the campus of Southwestern at Memphis. Outside the windows of the hall where we were planning this book, scores of lovely girls with bright pink and green bonnets, and scores of boys with peculiar placards on their backs, were streaming back and forth along the college walks. They were students of ten days' vintage, going through the struggles of Freshman Assimilation Period. They made an attractive pageant. But some of us kept wondering what was going on under those colorful bonnets and in front of those strange placards. Eager, no doubt, these young people were! And worried! And lonely! And excited! And full of great plans!

This was a critical time in their lives. Many of them, for the first time, were away from home and family, cast headlong into a world of fearsome sophomores and dignified seniors. All kinds of tests were facing them; all kinds of opportunities were before them. They must now re-think the ideas upon which their adolescent lives had been built. They must form new attitudes. Before long they must locate their niche in the work of the world. Now, if ever, they must find a faith that would be their own and that would hold them up.

College years are times of much loneliness, in spite of the fact that one is never away from the crowd. It is difficult for older people to remember the problems they faced in their days at college. It is a time of thrills, but often also a time of pain. These are years of adjustment to new freedoms, to groups of people, to larger ideas of life. In these years the student in sharpest fashion faces the tension in his own life—between the inevitable demand of his personality for the exercise of freedom, and the inescapable consciousness of dependence upon home and college and church. The first of these demands is to be encouraged. The college student is not yet an adult, but he is no longer a child. In these years the student is becoming a man or a woman. No one can become a strong adult or a competent Christian except as he becomes a free and independent personality in his thinking and in his moral decisions. But at the same time no one can become a well-balanced adult or a fully developed Christian without becoming happily adjusted to other personalities and to the institutions of the society in which he must find his satisfactions and to which he should make his contributions of service. Now he must learn what free decision means; now he must cultivate the art of friendship with people of different ages and outlooks; and now, above all, he must find a faith that will guide him in his decisions and that will enrich his associations.

These student years also are the critical years for the society from which these boys and girls come. More and more young people are finding a college education available to them. In a decade or so, education at the college level will be as common as high school education was thirty years ago. The increase in the number of college students has been from 50,000 in 1853, to 157,000 in 1890, and to more than two millions in 1955. Soon half of our young people may be able to go to college. In increasing measure, therefore, the leaders of tomorrow in state and church, in professions, in business and industry, will come from these men and women who have spent the formative years of their lives on college campuses. What happens to them during these critical years will go far toward deciding the future of our nation and its institutions. It will decide, too, in great measure, the effectiveness of the Church in the next generation.

These young people will receive training for all the tasks of

How can I discover
my talents?

On what basis should
I select my friends?

How should I choose
my lifework?

How much freedom
should I seek?

life. The information they receive and the skills they develop will be, if properly used, of the highest value. But the critical question concerns the effect of these college years on their moral insights and their spiritual attitudes. This will decide whether we are to have a world fit to live in. Indeed, it may decide whether we are to have any world left to live in at all. The attitudes with which these young people use powers available to them is critical for America and for the world. Apart from the spirit of Jesus Christ, America can never give the right answer. It is an answer beyond patriotism. Patriotism alone, unguided by Christian motives, may curse America and the world. The development of Christian faith during these college years is all-important. The influence of the Church upon the campus is crucial.

## The Church Must Understand Today's Students

There are certain factors in the experience of the student which we must understand if we are to help him in his growth.

1. These are the critical years because in them the student for the first time is *thrown on his own resources and must make his own decisions*. For the first time in any real sense these freshmen are leaving home. Many of them have been away for short trips or to summer camps. Some have gone to preparatory schools. But in camp and school they have been under rather close supervision. This is the first time the student can and must make most of his own decisions: when and how much he sleeps; when and how well he eats; how much time, if any, he gives to study. He is choosing his friends, either carelessly and on a superficial basis, or with a more thoughtful purpose. He is learning how to handle money to a degree that he has never had to do before. Now, for good or ill, he is forming habits that may be lifelong. Now in the stress of decision his character begins to strengthen or to falter. A week now may be as important as a year later on in his life.

The Church cannot make these decisions for him. It may, indeed, through our new vocational guidance centers, help him to come to a decision about his lifework. But if the Church cannot help the student with his particular decisions, it can throw about him an influence that will help to ensure that his decisions are made in a better way than if he were left alone.

The freshman's first week at college is possibly the most exciting week that he will ever spend. So many new experiences are flooding upon him. So many decisions have to be made, and in such a short time. All kinds of forces are pulling at him. There may never come a more important week in his life.

This is the time when the Church should meet him. All workers with students agree that the Church's first contact with the student is the most important one, and that the earlier that contact is made, the more it is likely to mean. In fact, the college town church should not wait for its preliminary contact until the student is on the campus. The student should discover at the start that the Church is one of the organizations that mean something in his life; that the Church is interested in him and wants to help him.

The Church's interest in the student should continue through his four years of undergraduate life and should follow him into graduate school. The freshman year is not the only difficult year. The senior year has its own special problems, particularly if the student has not by that time been able to decide upon his life-work. Many workers with students feel that the sophomore year is possibly the most dangerous of all. A college dean once spoke of the sophomore year as the "lost year." There is probably more peace of mind in the junior year than in any other. All along the way the student needs the sympathetic interest of the Church and the fellowship it can offer him.

2. These are the critical years because in them the student *is adjusting himself to life.* This is his first chance to face seriously the philosophy of life that has been given to him in his home. It is his first chance to revolt against it or to let it drift from him. It is his first real chance also to re-think it and make it his own. There are dangers in the fact that now as never before his life is his own. The cheap and the low will have their full chance to pull at him. Some of his new friends will tell him that he must be ready to try anything once. But if the Church keeps close to him there can be for him temptations upward also.

Sometimes the student faces an atmosphere of pseudosophistication, when the crowd makes a mock of his old standards. He is afraid above all things of seeming old-fashioned. The tendency is for him to become an average "College Joe." It is never easy at any age to stand out against the crowd; in adolescence it is the most difficult of all things to do. There is no more hazardous undertaking for the average college boy or girl than to try to be anything but average. One of the high possibilities of a good Westminster Fellowship is that it can give backing to students to stand out and be different.

Here the student has to make his early Church interest his own, or let it escape him. At home it is probable that his parents pressed him to go with them to services. At home many of his friends went; it was the natural thing to do. Now at college there may be no such compulsion, and there will be many influences drawing him away. There will be week-end trips and parties. There will be the pressure of studies, particularly when Saturday night has been given to pleasure. While church attendance may not be the major factor in holding to a vital religious faith, few people, in college or out of it, keep up a vital faith without the help of the Church. Consequently, among the other pressures of college life, the Church must keep up its friendly pressure upon the student.

3. These are the critical years because the student *is making new friends*. This again is one of the most exciting activities and one with the greatest possibilities for good or for harm. All who know students will agree that just as in the days of childhood the home is the dominant influence in a person's life, so during the college years student friendships have more effect on a boy or girl than any other force. There are few places where a strong personality can exert more influence upon other lives than on the college campus. Few college friendships may last over the years, but they are powerful while they last. The church is wise that provides for students the opportunity to form friendships in a student fellowship within the church's walls and under the church's influence.

4. These are the critical years because the student *is facing new ideas*. Before this time the interest of the boy or girl in a personal philosophy and in the meaning of the world in which he lives is largely academic. He is more concerned with activities and with immediate personal relationships. But in late adolescence his mind begins to inquire. The things he has always been told and which he has always taken for granted, he now begins to wonder about. "Are these things really true?" he asks. The very fact that these ideas have been given to him by others is a factor against his continued acceptance of them. It is a natural time of critical questioning. Some of this questioning would take place if he never went to college, but the atmosphere of college intensifies it. It should. After all, one of the primary reasons for college is to lead a youth to think, and then to guide him in his thinking.

As this inquiring individual enters the gates of college, he finds himself in an atmosphere of questioning. In the biological laboratory he looks through a microscope into the world of the infinitesimally small. In physics hall he looks through a telescope into a universe unbelievably large. In the sociology classroom he learns of human relationships far more complex than anything he has ever dreamed of. In dormitories, in fraternities and sororities, there are informal discussions that last half the night, in which everything on earth and in the heavens above and in the waters under the earth is canvassed. Many students, for help or hurt, learn more from fellow students than from faculty. In the classroom new ideas are opened up every hour. Visiting lecturers add to the ferment of thought and to the confusion of mind.

All of this is dangerous. Ideas always are. Ideas are far more dangerous than bullets. So much is this true that there are some colleges which, in an effort to help the student and control his thinking, deliberately try to deal out ideas sparingly and in a diluted form. There is said to be one college in the South that keeps a strict control, even off the campus, over the churches or lectures to which its students may go and the people whom they may visit. This college has a point. If its aim is to mold its students after its own likeness, and not after the likeness of freedom in Jesus Christ, it is taking the practical course. Ideas are dangerous; but minds without ideas are far more dangerous, for they are the prey of any dictator or demagogue who comes along with an ancient heresy.

But ideas are fruitful. Without them there can be no progress; without them there cannot even be any standing still. The nation or the Church that aims at thought control is on the way down, and therefore on the way out. Students are in the place where they can be learning to love the Lord their God with all their minds.

The Church's place is not to try to counterbalance the atmosphere of inquiry in which a student finds himself. The Church, if it is really to help students, will be in full sympathy with that atmosphere of freedom. The Church's help to the student in this area is twofold. It is, first, to furnish some of the basic ideas that should go into the making of the student's philosophy of life; the ideas which are not only themselves fundamental, but which are in turn fundamental to the proper use of any other ideas. It is the Church's business to provide the principles which alone—in an age when men have more knowledge than they have insight, more power than they have wisdom—will guide them into the high safety of righteousness and usefulness.

The second part of the Church's service is even more important. More than anything else, the student needs from the Church a fellowship in the atmosphere of faith and friendliness. Sometimes students feel helpless in the confusion of new ideas. Sometimes their supports are swept away; sometimes they are desperately lonely. A girl in one of our state schools in the South said to a worker who was discussing Christianity with her: "Why should anyone want to believe in immortality? One life is bad enough." Sir Walter Moberly in *The Crisis in the University* says that "the haunting trouble of the student today is a very deep-seated doubt whether in the modern world, so impersonal and so insecure, his life can have any significance. Existing university courses do little to reassure or to stimulate him."[1] For such students, and for all students, the Church needs to provide in the church near the campus and in the home of the worker with students a fellowship that is warm and that is built on the Christian faith.

## The Church Must Understand the Campus

There are elements in campus life today which seriously affect the lives of students and which, therefore, the Church should try to understand and to counteract or use. The effect of some of these tendencies is wholly good; the effect of others is largely hurtful; while in some of them there are possibilities both for good and for ill. Some of these tendencies seem to contradict each other. For example: along with an apparent tendency toward materialism in the outlook of students, there is a remarkable interest in the ministry as a life calling. This kind of contradiction reflects the confusion of our national life.

1. *There is the crowded nature of campus life.* The pressure of competing interests may not be any greater with college students than with adults in these busy days; but it does seem that students have less ability to discriminate, and consequently, a greater tendency to try to make a place for everything that comes. Where that is true, there is always the danger that religion will be pushed aside in favor of things more immediate in interest and with

greater pressure power. Fraternities are not going to stand back when they want a boy. Athletics will not be denied. Social life makes constant demands. For the spiritual life there is too often only the quiet call of conscience among a hundred claims.

A group of students agreed that as freshmen they began going to church out of a habit formed at home; that in the early months of college life there were not too many competing interests; but that by the time they had reached the middle of the first year they were much more occupied. Then, because it took a very positive desire to stick to the church, many dropped out. Some of them went on to say that by the senior year they were feeling the pressure of the deeper problems of life and the need of divine support, and so turned to the church again.

2. *Students appear to have a greater concern today with material rewards.* Most workers with students would agree that there is a more open and unashamed determination than ever before on the part of students in college to choose occupations which will bring in the quickest and largest possible financial returns. Unfortunately that is natural, for the campus reflects those contradictory elements in our American life that so puzzle observers from other lands: the strange combination of greed and generosity; the strenuous preoccupation with material concerns, and the surprising streaks of idealism that go along with this preoccupation. Certainly there has been among college students, as among all groups in our society, a growing concern with economic security. But while there is less idealistic talk among students, youth's old interest in service has not disappeared.

3. *An increasing number of students are coming from homes without religion.* We talk of holding our students for the Church, but we should realize that in many cases there is nothing to hold. Not a few of our students come from homes with only a nominal interest in the Church, or no interest at all. Once it was part of our technique to appeal to boys and girls on the basis of the faith of their ancestors and the piety of the homes which they had left. That appeal must now be made with caution.

We need to realize that with many students our task is purely evangelistic. They have never had a faith or a Church to be held for; they must be won to Christ from the beginning, and then built into the Church. One of our workers at a state college for women in the South drew into her Westminster Fellowship a girl whose parents had taught her that Christianity was a process of wishful thinking by which weaklings gained for themselves a sense of security and importance. But in the Church the girl found something that satisfied her hunger for reality. She became a loyal Christian. Against the ridicule of her family she stuck to her faith; and by her loyalty she achieved an influence on her campus.

Despite indications of greater materialism on our college campuses, a strong current of spiritual concern is making itself felt in other significant ways, such as those which follow:

5. *There is a steady improvement in the quality of American higher education.* This is certainly a debatable point; but the very fact of the widespread criticism of our higher education by educators themselves indicates a healthy condition. We who have lived long and who are in touch with campus life agree that students do more studying than in our own student days. The improvement in education is more evident in the technical fields than in liberal arts, but it is general. This means a more carefully trained leadership for our nation in future years. This, of course, is not enough. Improvement in the quality of our education is fine; but it does not necessarily carry improvement in the character and motives of the men and women who receive it. This can come only from clearer faith and more dedicated hearts. And this kind of improvement, although colleges and universities may help toward it, must come mainly from the Christian Church.

6. *There is a new interest on the part of students in the Church* and a new readiness to consider the place of the Church in their lives. Professor Gordon Allport in his *The Individual and Religion*, while pointing out the appalling ignorance on the part of students about Biblical and theological teachings, concludes that a majority of students today feel a genuine need for religious beliefs; that students are more religious in their practices than in their beliefs; and that there is some evidence that there has been an increase of religious faith since 1930. Most campus workers would think that his last statement is unduly cautious, at least so far as the South is

*Four years that make a difference.*
*Shall our Church help to shape them?*

concerned. They feel sure that more students are attending church and are interested in the church than for many student generations past. This trend began toward the end of World War II and showed itself first among veterans.

Twenty-five years ago the President of Oberlin, Dr. Ernest H. Wilkins, said to the Princeton Conference on Religion: "In a typical modern college body of 1,000 men there would be, I think, about 100 who might fairly be said to be religious-minded; rather more than 800 who would not ordinarily be concerned about religion, and a residuum who would consider themselves to have dispensed with religion." Those figures would certainly have to be revised today. The "residuum who would consider themselves to have dispensed with religion" would probably remain as large, but there has been a definite shift in the other figures. It would now be nearer one-third, and in not a few schools one-half, who have some real interest in religion. Practically all college workers would agree concerning this shift, although there would be a difference of opinion as to how deep the interest goes.

This increased interest in the Church is shown in a number of ways: in an increase in church attendance; in the number of courses on religion which are being introduced on all sides and in all kinds of institutions, and in the interest in such courses; in the increased effectiveness of campus Christian organizations; and in the number of students who are considering the ministry. It is risky to become too optimistic, but at least we can say that where formerly we were moving against the current, now we are beginning to move with it.

New interest on the part of students in the Church and its program is part of a general religious renaissance that is felt in our country. Dr. Elton Trueblood said recently: "Something of great excitement is going on in the religious life of our generation."[2] He mentioned such signs as eagerness for religious books, the great increase in the building of churches and church school plants, and the return of mass evangelism. The Church must do all in its power, under the direction of the Spirit of God, to see that this concern is deepened and made lasting.

7. Connected with this deeper interest in the Church is *a much greater concern among students about Christian beliefs*. In the early days of our century students who were interested in religion were primarily activists. They were busy in campus evangelism, in missions, and in various forms of social service. Students still want to share in these essential activities. They agree that service is a fundamental part of the Christian life. But the pressure in their minds today is ideological. They are awake to the warfare of philosophies in our world. They want to know what they should think about the great fundamentals of the Christian faith. The question that nearly always has first place in campus discussion groups is, "What should I think?" They want to hear about the sovereignty of God, about the Bible, about prayer, and above all about the meaning of Christ for the world and for their lives. There is a great ignorance among students about all these things, but a growing interest which gives the Church its opportunity to develop intelligent Christians.

8. *A much larger number of students are turning to the ministry as a life calling.* The increase is greater in state and independent institutions than in church colleges. These universities are sending more men to our seminaries every year of late. From the 1954 graduating class at Washington and Lee University five men went to Presbyterian seminaries, three to Episcopal, and one to a Baptist seminary. In one New England college dozens of men are headed for the ministry where a few years ago scarcely a man thought of such service.

Not infrequently men halfway or more through their scientific training in technical colleges are turning to the ministry, often surrendering considerable material prospects for the opportunity to serve Christ through the Church. To be sure, the number of men in such schools who do not go into the ministry but who go out to become active laymen in Christ's work is even more important; but it is a good thing for our seminaries not to have to depend entirely upon church schools for their recruits; and it is a good thing to have in the ministry some men who have had a more unconventional training than that of the regular liberal arts courses.

9. *There is a strong development of interest in religion and in the Church among faculty members.* To many this seems the most significant movement in the American educational field today. Its importance cannot be overestimated. American teachers are giving up their detached attitudes toward the Christian faith. There have always been many college professors who have sincerely believed in the Christian religion and who have quietly let their influence count. On the other hand, there have always been teachers who were frankly hostile. There still are men in both of these groups, but it is not too much to say that there is today on the part of faculty members in our colleges and universities a mounting wave of personal interest in Christianity. Dr. René Williamson* of Louisiana State University said recently to the Association of American Colleges that this faculty Christian movement is springing up spontaneously. It is a return, he said, "not

---

* In Chapter 7 Dr. Williamson gives a fuller account of this movement.

merely to religion, but to Christianity itself"; and is "a rediscovery of the Gospel in an age of moral and ideological confusion." It has not been induced by a special effort on the part of the churches; it is self-initiated, and spreads from teacher to teacher and from college to college. It is just as true of state institutions as of church colleges, and is perhaps more noticeable in the former.

This development will have its effect in the classroom. Christian professors will be careful not to transgress the bounds of classroom propriety in the handling of religion—more careful, probably, than hostile professors have been. This awakened interest means that the relation of many fields to the Christian faith will be dealt with more respectfully and that there will be more patience with and more positive guidance for students as they face new truth. We have no right to ask that Christianity be taught in the literary and scientific classroom; we do have the right to expect that Christianity will be treated with respect and consideration.

10. *Do not forget the married students.* One of the greatest changes in the campus scene is in the "pre-fab" village, or in some cases the substantial dormitories for married couples. A decade ago the married student, except in the graduate school, was a curiosity; now he is a commonplace. Those of us who live around campuses will never forget the lifting of academic eyebrows when the veterans of World War II began to bring their brides under the shelter of the ivied walls. "There will be no more studying!" the faculty wailed. "The ivory towers will be shaken down." Now, the only thing that has been shaken down is the fear about the women. There is almost unanimous agreement that married men are doing the more serious studying. The men themselves have a clearer sense of duty; and where that begins to lag, the wives have enough for both. Financially there have been problems, although, up to the coming of the first baby, working wives have been found to be an asset: there is a catchword, "working one's way through school by the sweat of his frau." For the time being at least, the young family is a definite institution around the modern campus.

## The Church Must Follow Her Students

We have seen that the student needs the Church. Just as truly *the Church needs the students.* A large part of our able and trained leadership in the next generation must come from these men and women now in college. If our Christianity is to be taken out of the seclusion of the churches and translated into actuality where men and women live and work and struggle, it must be done by these college students. If we want Christianity to become an effective force in the life of our nation and of the world, we need these students.

*The Church must keep close to her students while they are in college.* We must do this in part by providing church colleges which are, not merely in name but in reality, *Christian colleges.* They must be colleges that are good enough to command intellectual respect. They must be small enough to provide close contacts between students and the most important men and women on the faculties. They must be so truly Christian that students will be kept in touch with Christ and the Church.

We must keep this close contact with students by *following those who go to the state institutions.** We must make an adequate preaching ministry possible on every campus. College students need preaching of a high type. They need preaching that is intelligent and that will meet them on their own level, by a minister who will know enough not to lug into his preaching too much of science and philosophy but who will understand these things well enough to command the respect of students. They need preaching that is spiritual, with an understanding of the needs of men and of the grace of God. They need preaching that is warm and compelling, that sets men in the face of the challenge and the power of the living Christ.

We must provide a Westminster Fellowship program that will give students the opportunity for Christian development and activity. The basic principle in the campus Christian life philoso-

---

* The Campus Christian Life movement of the Presbyterian Church in the United States will be discussed in more detail in Chapter 6.

phy of our Church is that students need to be built into a normal church life. The program will be helpful to the degree in which it treats them not as peculiar beings but as normal church members.

All the things that have been discussed in this chapter—the factors in the student's changing life that make the college years critical, and the elements in his campus environment—point up the need for a thoughtful and aggressive program on the part of the Church to reach the student and to help him.

CHAPTER

## FRANCIS PICKENS MILLER

A.B., Washington and Lee University; B.A. and M.A., Oxford University in England; Rhodes Scholar.

Chairman, World's Student Christian Federation, Geneva, Switzerland, 1928-38.

Field Secretary, Foreign Policy Association, 1934-35. Secretary, National Policy Association, 1935-38; vice-chairman, 1938-42. Secretary, Southern Policy Association, 1935-40.

Organization Director, Council on Foreign Relations, 1938-42.

Member, Virginia House of Delegates, 1938-41.

Formerly member, Boards of Visitors of St. John's College, College of William and Mary, and of the United States Military Academy, West Point. Member of Board of Trustees of Mary Baldwin College.

Candidate for governor of Virginia, 1949, and for U. S. senator, 1952.

Lieutenant-Colonel, Army of the United States, 1943, and Colonel, General Staff Corps, 1945. In military government at Berlin, 1945-46. Numerous decorations, including Legion of Merit with Oak Leaf Cluster, Legion of Honor, Order of British Empire, Croix de Guerre.

Member, Central Committee, World Council of Churches, 1955.

Author and co-author of several books.

# For Dignity of Man and Glory of God

## PRESBYTERIAN COLLEGES AND HUMAN LIBERTY

### by *Francis Pickens Miller*

GOD created man for responsible freedom. But freedom is not a gift. It has to be earned. Every free society secured its freedom at a great price—the price of toil, blood, and unceasing vigilance. Hence it is not surprising that the Christian religion has been the principal source of human liberty as we know it in the West, since this faith not only inspires men to seek freedom but makes them willing to pay the price necessary to secure it.

The forces which fashion human society are so complex that the greatest scholar cannot fully understand and describe them. Yet it is possible at times to name certain places and individuals that have played a decisive part in originating world-transforming movements. It is also possible occasionally to trace these movements down through the centuries.

### The Academy of Geneva: Fountainhead of Human Liberty Under God's Sovereignty

Human liberty as we know it in the United States can be traced back to many origins. But among all these origins one place, one man, one form of religion, and one institution have pre-eminence. The place is Geneva, Switzerland, during the latter half of the sixteenth century. The man is John Calvin, who made Geneva his base of operations. The religion is the Reformed faith, with its representative system of church government. The institution is the Academy of Geneva, founded by Calvin in 1559, which became in due course the University of Geneva.

The central affirmation of John Calvin and his associates was what he called the "sovereignty" of God. This means that God runs the world and that the government is upon His shoulders. As Christians we are citizens by faith of a realm which overarches the governments and empires of this world. And our citizenship in God's Realm determines what kind of Genevans, what kind of Scotsmen, what kind of Englishmen, and what kind of Americans we can be. This is the inescapable logic of Calvin's teaching.

In his *Institutes*, Calvin wrote: "We are subject to the men who rule over us, but subject only in the Lord. If they command anything against Him, let us not pay the least regard to it, nor be moved by all the dignity which they possess as magistrates."[1] That is revolutionary doctrine. It implies that each thinking man with a conscience has as much right as a king to ask which laws or institutions are in harmony with or contrary to the will of God. And as soon as men successfully assert their right to question those who govern them, they have become free men.

The strength of the Reformed religion in the sixteenth century lay in the fact that its doctrine was not just theoretical speculation but was expressed in the structure and procedures of church organization. A representative system of church government was inherent in the doctrine and came into being wherever the Reformed religion prevailed. The impact of the Reformed religion with its representative system of church government free from state control prepared the way for the transformation of the structure of Western society and the establishment of civil and religious freedom.

John Knox returned to Scotland from exile in Geneva in 1559 and the following year established the first national church with the Presbyterian form of government. In 1561, the implications of the new religion for human liberty were succinctly given in a reply Knox made to Mary, Queen of Scots. The Queen asked, "Think ye that subjects, having power, may resist their princes?"

Knox answered, "If their princes exceed their bounds, Madam, they may be resisted and even deposed." Two hundred years later, this view had become the accepted political creed of the overwhelming majority of colonists in the new world called America.

Calvin's doctrine required a representative system of church government. It also required a system of general education, including languages and the "arts," as well as theology. It was obvious that ministers of the Reformed Church had to be well educated. But it was also implicit in Reformed doctrine that laymen who assumed the responsibilities of free citizens had to be equally well educated.

Calvin believed that true faith must be intelligent; that intelligence and not ignorance was the mother of piety; and consequently, that the school was an essential part of any effective church organization. Having these convictions, Calvin, upon his return from Strassburg to Geneva in 1541, announced the establishment of a school system as one of his primary objectives. However, it took him nearly as long to achieve this objective as it took Jefferson to realize his dream of a University of Virginia. It was not until 1559 (just a few years before his death) that the Academy of Geneva was established. There were two departments—a secondary or preparatory department, and a department of higher education which included courses in Latin, Greek, Hebrew, philosophy or "arts," and theology. Shortly after Calvin's death, courses in law and medicine were added.

Calvin was as proud of the Academy of Geneva as Jefferson was of the University of Virginia. Like Jefferson, he regarded the founding of the Academy as the crowning work of his life and intended that it should become the intellectual center of the Reformed world. From it hundreds of trained ministers, theologians, and scholars went forth to France and other countries where the Reformation was at work. From it also went hundreds of laymen to spread Reformed doctrine and to put the implications of that doctrine into effect in the affairs of state.

For a century after Calvin's death the movement which he launched was the most potent force in the development of civil liberty throughout the Western world. In this development, the

Academy of Geneva played a unique role—particularly as far as the English-speaking countries were concerned. Of course, the Academy itself was not consciously in the business of overthrowing monarchies and creating democratic governments in their place. But more than any other single institution, it molded the men who laid the foundations for free societies in England, Scotland, and America.

## The Stream Flows to Virginia

The story of the influence of Geneva and its Academy upon the course of Western civilization has never been fully told. All we can do in this chapter is to sketch in brief outline two streams of its influence and mention some of the persons through whom this influence found expression. The reader must bear in mind that, important as were the individuals mentioned here, scores and even hundreds of others, equally influenced by Geneva, played their allotted parts in the vast drama of human liberty that unfolded between 1550 and 1800.

The first part of our story leads from the Academy of Geneva through England to Virginia. The second part leads from the Academy through Scotland to New Jersey. And finally, the two streams of influence originating in Geneva unite in creative fulfillment at the College of New Jersey, in the sessions of the Continental Congress, on the floor of the Constitutional Convention of 1787, and in the Constitution of the United States.

Soon after the Academy of Geneva was founded, it became a mecca for freedom-loving young men from England and Scotland and as a result exercised a decisive influence on the life of Great Britain from the reign of Elizabeth to the end of the Cromwellian period. Heylyn wrote, "In the latter part of the 16th and early in the 17th centuries many English youth were sent to Geneva to study the Reformed Religion out of an opinion which their parents have that it is no where so purely practised and professed as there. And thus being seasoned with Genevan principles have many times proved disaffected to the forms of government (as well monarchical as Episcopal) which they found established here at home." To list the names of these students would be to call a roll of men who later became leaders in putting an end to absolute monarchy in Scotland and England.

## Edwin Sandys' Life Is Shaped at Geneva

We are concerned here with two of these students. The first is Edwin Sandys of England. Sandys was born in 1561, son of Edwin Sandys, the first Protestant Archbishop of York. He was educated at Merchant Taylor's School, London, and at Corpus Christi College, Oxford. From 1586 to 1593, he was a member of Parliament and then left England for six years of travel on the Continent. On November 6, 1597, he registered as a student at the Academy in Geneva. The impression made upon him by Geneva—by the lectures he heard in the Academy and by what he saw of the government of the city—changed the whole course of his life. More than twenty years later, in the midst of the climactic struggle of his career with James I, he was heard to say: "If our God from Heaven did constitute and direct a forme of Government on Earth it was that of Geneva." When he returned to England he carried with him an attitude of skepticism toward the absolute power of monarchs and a growing preference for democratic institutions.

In 1603, Sandys went to Edinburgh to meet James VI of Scotland and to accompany him as he traveled toward London to become James I of England as well as James VI of Scotland. Though Sandys was immediately knighted by James, the era of good feeling between the two was of short duration.

Sandys once more became a member of Parliament and was a dominant figure during the session of 1604, serving for some years thereafter as the leader of an independent party in the House of Commons. He frequently spoke on behalf of the interests of the people as over against the Crown, insisted that all prisoners should have the right to employ counsel, and attacked the great monopolies. He helped draft for the House of Commons its remonstrance against the conduct of James I toward his first Parliament, and he is reported to have done so "with great force of reasoning and Spirit of Liberty." In replying to this remonstrance, James told the members of the House, "You have done many things rashly." For the next twenty years, Sandys and the king were

John Calvin

Edwin Sandys

John Witherspoon

Moses Hoge

constantly at loggerheads. In 1613 Sandys enunciated the revolutionary principle that there were certain reciprocal conditions of the Constitution which neither king nor people might violate with impunity. The struggle between Sandys and James I was a struggle between the growing desire among many Englishmen for more liberty and the assertion by the Stuart kings of the absolute authority of the monarch.

This struggle found its more dramatic expression in the policies of the London Company for Virginia. Sandys became a member of that Company and, from the first, represented the "popular" point of view as over against the position of the king's men. The initial settlements in Virginia were made under a charter which gave the king direct control of the colony. This arrangement had not worked well, and the colonists petitioned the king to transfer the government of the colony to the London Company. James agreed to do so, and in 1609 Sandys wrote a new popular charter for Virginia including a guarantee of the "inalienable rights of freeborn Englishmen" to which Virginians were to appeal when they broke away from another royal form of government one hundred and sixty-seven years later.

Sandys' training at the Academy of Geneva was beginning to bear fruit. So far, he had done little more than sketch the faint outlines of the grand design he had in mind for creating a free popular state in Virginia along the lines of what he had seen in Geneva. For the next twelve years, it was his constant aim to effect gradual changes in the Virginia charters that would make them more and more favorable to the Company and to the colony. As he slowly and surely accomplished his purpose, it was evident— at least to his enemies—that he kept in mind the government of Geneva as the model of independence and liberty from which he had drawn his inspiration. In 1618 he drafted a concrete proposal for submission to the London Company. This plan was adopted and a government was agreed upon, consisting of (1) The Council of State composed of the Governor and his Counsellors elected by the Company court in England, and (2) The General Assembly composed of the aforementioned Council of State and two Burgesses chosen out of each Town Hundred or other particular Plantation by the people of Virginia. As Treasurer of the

Company during 1619-1620 Sandys was in a strategic position to help put these plans into effect.

A new governor, Sir George Yeardley, had been appointed by the Company, and when he arrived in Virginia he made a momentous announcement to the colonists:

> And that they might have a hand in the governing of themselves, it was granted that a General Assembly should be held yearly once, whereat were to be present the Governor and Counsell, with two Burgesses from each Plantation freely to be elected by the inhabitants thereof; this Assembly to have power to make and ordaine whatsoever lawes and orders should by them be thought good and profittable for our subsistence.

This General Assembly was the first popular representative governing body ever held in the Western Hemisphere. It convened at Jamestown on August 9, 1619. Thus Sandys' great experiment of a "free state" in the New World got under way.

As a part of his policy of making Virginia a colony where civil and religious liberty would prevail, Sandys had begun in 1617 to correspond with his old friend Elder William Brewster regarding the possibility of the Pilgrims leaving Leyden and going to Virginia. After lengthy negotiations, the patent for the Pilgrims' settlement in Virginia was duly approved and sealed by the London Company, and was sent by Brewster to Leyden. Owing to a long and rough crossing of the North Atlantic, the *Mayflower* by mistake came to Cape Cod rather than to Chesapeake Bay, but this misadventure should not be allowed to obscure the fact that it was only because of the liberal policies of the London Company for Virginia that the Pilgrims were allowed to set sail for the New World. And the privileges of government enshrined in "the Mayflower compact" of November 21, 1620, were granted to the Pilgrims by the popular charters of Virginia under which they had been sent to that colony.

It was inevitable, of course, that as soon as the system of representative government introduced into Virginia by the London Company clashed with the system of absolute authority preferred by James I, the latter would temporarily prevail. The clash was not long in coming. During the spring of 1620 the king decided to deny to the court of the London Company the right granted to have a free election of its own officers. In reply to a protest from the Company, which desired to re-elect Sandys as its treasurer, James I on May 29 declared Sandys to be his "greatest enemy," and in a furious passion told the Company to "choose the Devil if you will, but not Sir Edwin Sandys."

On June 26, 1621, Sandys was arrested by the king's orders and his house searched for papers. According to the *British Dictionary of National Biography*, Sandys, who in 1618 had organized the government of Virginia and introduced an era of prosperity, was now imprisoned in the Tower of London on suspicion of designing to establish a republican and puritan state in America. It was also said that "Sandys was arrested for having spoken in Parliament in defense of the Liberty of the subject."

It was evident that James I had decided to annul the popular charters for Virginia as soon as he could find an occasion for doing so, and bring the control of Virginia back under the Crown. By 1623, matters had come to a head. The king appointed a commission to report to him on the affairs of the London Company. The popular leaders were arrested (including Sandys for the second time), and Lord Southampton, Governor of the Virginia Courts, was by the king's direction confined to his house. The leaders of Sandys' party having been silenced, the Privy Council in the autumn of 1623 issued orders to the settlers in Virginia that their popular charters were to be surrendered and that the government of the colony was to be returned to the king without any provision for a House of Burgesses or a General Assembly. Thirty members of the General Assembly of Virginia replied in a letter to the Privy Council:

> We humblie desire that the Governors that are sent over may not have absolute authority. We desire that the Governor may be restrayned as formerly to the consent of his Counsell . . . But above all we humbly intreat your Lordships that we may retaine the Libertie of our General Assemblie, than which nothing can more conduce to our satisfaction or the publique utilitie.

The Virginians were so firm in their determination not to accept the abolition of their General Assembly, and the members of Sandys' party in the London Company so stubborn in their refusal to give an inch more to the king than they were compelled to give, that events moved slowly and the Royal Commission had not yet reported its recommendations for a new charter when James I suddenly died on April 6, 1625. The Commission and its proposals expired with the king. So Charles I had to make a new beginning, and to show his good will the Privy Council called the Sandys party into consultation. The result of all this was that although the Crown resumed the government of Virginia as James I had desired, in the autumn of 1627 Charles I consented to the continuance of the House of Burgesses to be elected as formerly, by the people. By establishing representative government in Virginia, Sir Edwin Sandys had planted the tree of Liberty in the New World, and the tree had taken root and begun to grow.

The Virginia House of Burgesses was the university of civil liberty from which George Mason, George Washington, Thomas Jefferson, and James Madison went forth to take the government of the colonies from the Crown, to restore it to the people, and to found a free, popular state in America. Thus they carried forward to completion the work initiated by Edwin Sandys, Englishman and alumnus of John Calvin's Academy of Geneva. Education and love of liberty moved together.

## The Stream Flows to New Jersey

We have been following one of the streams of influence that flowed out from Geneva in the late sixteenth century. Now let us turn to another stream that flowed from there through Scotland to New Jersey.

John Knox returned to Scotland in 1559 from his exile in Geneva. It was in Geneva that he had learned that God had given people certain rights which neither king nor pope could take away.

The year that Knox returned, a fourteen-year-old lad, Andrew Melville, entered St. Andrews University as a student. After completing his courses there Melville, like many Scots of his day, went to France in 1564 to continue his studies at Paris and Poitiers. Because it was becoming increasingly difficult for Protestants to move about in France, Melville decided to make his way to

Geneva and succeeded in gaining entrance in 1569 to that refuge of adherents to the Reformed religion. Calvin had been dead five years, and his Academy was just ten years old. In spite of Melville's youth (he was only twenty-four), the brilliance of his mind and his wealth of learning earned him a welcome by Theodore Beza and an appointment to the Chair of Humanity in the Academy, a position which he occupied for the next five years.

In 1574, inspired and armed by his ten years on the Continent and particularly by his experience in Geneva, Melville returned to Scotland and immediately plunged into the struggles which engaged him for the rest of his life.

While principal of the University of Glasgow (1574-1580), Melville took a leading part in the overthrow of Episcopacy and the substitution of Presbytery as the form of government for the Church in Scotland. He regarded his efforts in this cause as the most valuable service he could render his country. Mainly because of Melville's exertions, the Second Book of Discipline, containing the authorized form of representative government for the Church of Scotland which has continued to this day, was adopted at the 1578 meeting of the General Assembly in Edinburgh, of which Melville was Moderator.

At the same time, the Assembly was concerned with the reformation and remodeling of all the Scottish universities, and particularly with transforming one of the colleges of St. Andrews into a theological seminary. In order to get this done, Melville was transferred to St. Andrews from Glasgow in 1580, when he became principal of New College.

His activities on behalf of establishing a representative form of government in the Church inevitably brought Melville into conflict with James VI (later James I of England). In 1584 he was called before the Privy Council to answer for treasonable statements made in a sermon and was condemned to imprisonment in the "death cell" Castle of Blackness, but he managed to escape to England and remained in London until James VI acquired less hostile favorites. The goal of Melville's life was realized in 1592 when the Scottish Parliament passed an act establishing the Presbyterian form of church government in Scotland. This was his greatest achievement. Two years later, he became for the third time Moderator of the General Assembly.

From 1594 the conflict between James VI and Melville steadily worsened. Finally, in 1606, three years after James had become king of both England and Scotland, Melville and seven other Scottish ministers were summoned to London in order "that his Majesty might treat with them of such things as would tend to settle the peace of the church." The ministers told James that the only solution was to call a *free* General Assembly. Shortly afterward Melville was committed to the Tower of London, where he remained for four years. When released, he accepted a professor's chair at Sedan in France, and died there in 1622. Next to John Knox, Scotland owed most to Andrew Melville.

James VI of Scotland and I of England was absolutely right when he said at the Hampton Court Conference in 1604: "A Scottish Presbytery as well agreeth with a Monarchy, as God and the Devill. Then Jacke, and Tom, and Will and Dick shall meet, and at their pleasures censure me and my Councell and all our proceedings." The General Assembly of the Church in Scotland, as well as the General Assembly of the Plantation in Virginia, represented forces of the human spirit which were irresistible, and against which such doctrines as the divine right of kings could do no more than fight a brief delaying action.

A hundred years after Andrew Melville died, another Scot was born to carry on the same unending struggle for human liberty. This was John Witherspoon, who was educated at the University of Edinburgh. He completed his theological studies in 1743. He was heir to all that Melville had accomplished and to the seventeenth-century victories of the General Assembly of the Church over the dictatorial claims of the monarchy. Shortly after he became minister at Beith, his passion for freedom and his ability as a controversialist found an opportunity for expression during 1745, when the young Pretender made his abortive attempt to restore the Stuarts to the throne of Scotland. For more than twenty years, Witherspoon was one of the most popular preachers in the country; but in 1768 he accepted a second invitation to become president of the struggling little college at Princeton, New Jersey, which subsequently became Princeton University. Before leaving Scotland, he had already proved himself to be a "stedfast opponent of entrenched authority" whether in church or state.

Upon arrival in New Jersey, Witherspoon identified himself completely with the American cause, and became one of the stoutest advocates of independence. One of the subjects on which he began to lecture was "The Law of Nature and of Nations," which led into the whole field of social and political organization. He converted the parochial College of New Jersey (as Princeton was then called) into a cultural center which drew students from the entire eastern seaboard. He added Hebrew and French to the curriculum, provided scientific equipment, organized graduate courses, and set out immediately on a quest for more funds and more students.

Witherspoon was as active in his church as in his college. In due course he took the lead in bringing Presbyterians together in one General Assembly, of which he was the first Moderator.

But Witherspoon's most valuable service to America was the part he played in encouraging the colonists to achieve their independence, and then to establish an enduring republic. He did this by his own active participation in public affairs, as well as through the students whom he trained and sent out from his college. Because of his Calvinist background, Witherspoon was well aware that theological and philosophical ideas would become sterile unless related to the living issues of the day. Consequently, he threw himself with zest into the American struggle for religious and civil liberty. When people said the time was not yet ripe for a Declaration of Independence, Witherspoon replied, "In my judgment the country is not only ripe for the measure but in danger of becoming rotten for the want of it." He headed a local Committee of Correspondence, organized a military company in the college, was a member of two provincial congresses and of the New Jersey Constitutional Convention, and for five years was a member of the Continental Congress. John Adams of Massachusetts paid him the tribute of calling him "as high a son of liberty as any man in America." In the course of a sermon in Princeton on May 17, 1776, Witherspoon had declared, "There is not a single instance in history in which civil liberty was lost and religious liberty preserved entire . . . He is the best friend to American Liberty, who is the most sincere and active in promoting true and undefiled religion— God grant that in America true religion and civil liberty may be inseparable and that the unjust attempts to destroy the one may in the issue tend to the support and establishment of both."[2] He was the only clergyman to sign the Declaration of Independence.

Just as John Witherspoon favored a General Assembly to provide a central representative government for the Presbyterian Church, so he realized the urgent need for a stronger central government if the Confederation was to survive. He was a member of every important committee of the Continental Congress and interestingly enough made his most valuable contributions in the fields of Supply and Finance, publishing an "Essay on Money" which was highly regarded for the soundness of the views expressed. At the darkest moment of the war, during the winter of 1776 and 1777, Witherspoon realized that desperate measures were required to sustain the confidence of the people and prevent capitulation. Consequently, he was one of those who encouraged Tom Paine to write the thirteen papers called "The Crisis," the first of which began, "These are times that try men's souls. The summer soldier and the sunshine patriot will, in this crisis, shrink from the service of their country." These papers were some of the most powerful, the most successful, and the most inexpensive propaganda ever released in America. Because of the value of Paine's contribution, Witherspoon stood by him and aided him in every way he could in spite of the former's irresponsible character.

Great as were Witherspoon's personal services to the American cause, of even greater value was the contribution made by the students of his college. The College of New Jersey had become a rallying point for young patriots before Witherspoon's arrival from Scotland, and by the time the first Continental Congress was called in Philadelphia, the president, the faculty, and all the students were "Sons of Liberty." It is no exaggeration to say that under Witherspoon's direction the tiny college at Princeton, with a student body of fewer than a hundred, served the cause of human liberty in America in the last third of the eighteenth century in somewhat the same way that its institutional ancestor, the Academy of Geneva, had served the cause of human liberty in Western Europe during the latter half of the sixteenth century. Princeton became in a unique sense a Liberty Hall of the American colonies.

Two former students of Princeton, in addition to its president, signed the Declaration of Independence. Twenty-eight alumni served in the Continental Congress, and more than a hundred on local committees of correspondence, in provincial constitutional conventions and congresses, or as officials of newly created state governments. During the Revolutionary War, more than two hundred Princetonians served in the Army, including "Light Horse Harry" Lee, James Caldwell, the Fighting Parson, and Joseph Reed, military secretary to General Washington. Princeton furnished to the infant Republic from classes prior to 1800 a Chief Justice of the Supreme Court and four Associate Justices, five Secretaries of State, four Secretaries of the Treasury, three Secretaries of the Navy, a Secretary of War, a Postmaster General, and four Attorneys General. In addition, the classes prior to 1800 supplied thirty-three senators and sixty representatives to the Federal Congress.

## Presbyterianism and the American Form of Government

This chapter began with Geneva and journeyed through England to Virginia and through Scotland to New Jersey; but our story is not yet ended. For the confluence of these two streams of influence had a decisive effect on the form of government through which man's aspiration for religious and civil liberty was to express itself in the New World.

James Madison, Senior, of Virginia had made a contribution to the College of New Jersey and this is perhaps one reason he sent his son James to Princeton. The younger Madison may also have been attracted to Princeton because he was thinking of becoming a minister. But probably the main attraction of Princeton was the reputation it had already acquired as a center of revolutionary thought.

After his graduation in 1771, Madison asked his father to allow him to stay for an additional six months of study directly under the supervision of John Witherspoon, who had great affection for him. This juxtaposition of John Witherspoon and young James Madison was no ordinary event. We see, on the one hand, the forty-seven-year-old college president, bearer of the tradition of the General Assembly of the Church of Scotland and heir to John Calvin's Geneva through John Knox and Andrew Melville; and on the other, the eighteen-year-old youth, bearer of the tradition of the General Assembly of Virginia and heir of John Calvin's Geneva through Edwin Sandys. When these two men were brought together in a common search for truth, it was inevitable that great ideas and great proposals should result from the impact of their minds and personalities. Without his knowing it, the young Madison was being educated for a decisive role in the drama of freedom that was beginning to unfold.

After returning to Virginia in 1772, Madison continued his studies and lived quietly for several years because of his health. But in 1775 he became chairman of the committee of public safety in Orange County and for the next forty years participated in the great events of his day as a member, successively, of the Virginia Convention, the Council of State of Virginia, the Continental Congress, the Virginia House of Delegates, the Constitutional Convention of 1787, the Virginia Convention of 1788, and the Federal House of Representatives. He was Secretary of State under Jefferson, and succeeded the latter as President.

It was on Madison's initiative that Commissioners from Virginia and Maryland met at Alexandria and Mount Vernon in 1785. This paved the way for the Annapolis Convention of 1786, which led to the Philadelphia Constitutional Convention of 1787. The "Virginia Plan" for a new system of government had been drafted by Madison, and this became the basis for the Convention's deliberations which ended with the adoption of the Constitution of the United States on September 17. Madison was one of the three authors of the Federalist Papers explaining and advocating the new Constitution. Perhaps his greatest triumph was in his direction and conduct of the debate in the Virginia Convention of 1788 which finally ratified the Federal Constitution, although public opinion was at first against it and it was opposed in the Convention by Patrick Henry, George Mason, James Monroe, Benjamin Harrison, and John Tyler.

Future generations were to call James Madison "The Father of the Constitution." And so he was. Through him and his associates, the dream of Edwin Sandys had finally been realized more than a century and a half after Sandys' own efforts to realize his dream had appeared to be a complete failure. A "free state" had been erected in the New World as a beacon of hope for all men everywhere.

We Presbyterians are in a unique sense the heirs of this great heritage of human liberty. Our institutions of higher education in Geneva, in Scotland, and in New Jersey had made many of the men who made this free society.

Presbyterians in the American colonies during the last half of the eighteenth century were well aware of the relationship between higher education and the preservation of human liberty. Consequently, they were determined to create the educational institutions which could be relied upon to continue to serve the cause of freedom in the years ahead. In all of their principal settlements colleges were established.

In the Valley of Virginia, Presbyterians founded a Liberty Hall near Lexington (now Washington and Lee University); in North Carolina they organized two Liberty Halls and took the lead in founding the University of North Carolina; in Georgia and Tennessee they started the schools which eventually became the University of Georgia and the University of Tennessee; in South Carolina they established Zion Academy at Winnsboro; and in Kentucky they founded Transylvania. Then there was Hampden-Sydney, founded in 1776 by James Madison, Patrick Henry, and Colonel Carrington to serve the cause of liberty in Virginia as Princeton had done in New Jersey. It has a noble tradition and has contributed many famous men to American life. Davidson, Southwestern at Memphis, Centre College of Kentucky, and Agnes Scott are among the finest liberal arts colleges in the South, and we are justly proud of them as well as of our other institutions of higher education.

It is obvious that in the earlier days Presbyterians knew the meaning of responsible freedom and were aware of the obligations which their Christian faith laid upon them as citizens. Nor is it surprising that in London the Revolution was called "a Presbyterian rebellion" and that Bancroft the historian later wrote: "The first voice publicly raised in America to dissolve all connections with Great Britain came . . . from the Presbyterians."

Why, in the twentieth century, have so many people who call themselves Presbyterians lost that sense of obligation to express their faith in political action? Can it be that we no longer believe what Calvin and Knox and Melville and Sandys and Witherspoon believed?

The survival of liberty can never be taken for granted. Its survival in the United States, as elsewhere, depends upon whether there are vital centers of higher education that will serve the same function in the years ahead that the Academy of Geneva served in the last half of the sixteenth century and that Princeton served in the last half of the eighteenth century.

We have some grand colleges in our Presbyterian Church, U. S. But a haunting question remains and demands an answer: Are our church colleges now making men and women who in their day will see to it that human liberty continues to triumph in the life of America? Are we Presbyterians supporting these colleges on such a scale and with such enthusiasm that they have the means to accomplish the purposes for which they were founded? The answer to the latter question is a humiliating "no." By and large, we have lost interest in maintaining colleges to do what the Academy of Geneva or Princeton did. Financial support of any institution is the surest gauge of public interest in it. And the pitiful contributions which our Presbyterian Church as such has made to many of its colleges in recent years is convincing proof that most of us no longer regard Presbyterian higher education as essential to the survival of human liberty. If civil and religious freedom shall have ceased to exist in America a hundred years from now, we Presbyterians will be more to blame than any other people. But there is still time—if we will arouse ourselves and act as our fathers did in the sixteenth and eighteenth centuries.

## CHAPTER 3

## *ROBERT TODD LAPSLEY LISTON*

President, King College, 1943—

A.B., Davidson College, 1920.

B.D., Union Theological Seminary, 1924, and Th.M., 1925.

Ph.D., University of Edinburgh, Scotland, 1930.

Assistant professor of Hebrew, Union Theological Seminary, 1927-28.

Pastor, Richlands, Va., 1928-37.

Associate professor of Bible, Southwestern at Memphis, 1937-40.

President, Davis and Elkins College, 1940-43.

# Blood, Sweat, and Prayers

## HOW PRESBYTERIANS BUILT THEIR COLLEGES

## *by R. T. L. Liston*

### Calvin Points the Way

THE national character of the United States was fixed before its settlement—fixed not by national genes or racial inheritances, but by religious and educational influences. Rufus Choate tells us:

> In the reign of Mary, from 1553 to 1558, a thousand learned Englishmen fled from the stake at home to the happier states of continental Protestantism. Of these, great numbers—I know not how many—came to Geneva. . . . I ascribe to that five years in Geneva an influence which has changed the history of the world. I seem to myself to trace to it, as an influence on the English race, a new theology; new politics; another tone of character; the opening of another era of time and of liberty. I seem to myself to trace to it the great Civil War of England; the Republican Constitution framed in the cabin of the Mayflower; the divinity of Jonathan Edwards; the Battle of Bunker Hill; the independence of America.[1]

The Protestant Reformation taught the authority and power of God with a new vividness, producing a new conscience, a new strength, a new individuality in personal life, a new independence and initiative in business, a new spirit of democracy in political affairs. If we must name one man as responsible for this, we are bound to think of John Calvin, and to say of him as a German professor did, that here was a Frenchman who had more influence on the English-speaking world than any Englishman or any American who ever lived.*

We are bound to know that this commanding influence was due largely to the prowess of Calvin as a scholar and educator, and to the standards of intellectual life and educational zeal which became so characteristic of Calvinism.

These Calvinists, when they came to America, brought with them all this love of liberty, all these traits of character, and the certainty that these things had been developed by the Church and by its educational program. They believed that the Church as they knew it, and loved it, could not survive without its educational work.

This awareness of the dependence of the church and the community upon Christian educational institutions dominated the earliest educational efforts in America and led the settlers to sacrifice for it. We read that in the "starving time" one man gave a calf, another gave a bushel of potatoes, and another gave a half bushel of wheat to one of these early colleges. The power and permanence of their religion, their economic initiative, and their personal and political independence, seemed all bound together in a mutual dependence upon education.

These were Calvinist ideas. The attitude of the Crown and its established Church was expressed by one of its colonial governors in 1674: "I thank God there are no free schools nor printing, and I hope we shall not have these hundred years; for learning has brought disobedience into the world and libels against the best government, and printing hath divulged them! God keep us from both!"‡ It was the Presbyterians, and their inseparable brethren the Congregationalists, who could lift their faces against this and say, "It is the policy of the Presbyterian Church to foster institutions of higher learning under her care." The Congregationalists gave us Harvard and Yale. The Presbyterians struggled with their log colleges and finally built the "College of New Jersey," now

---

* Chapter 2 gives a fuller treatment of the influence of Calvin's Geneva.

‡ Reproduced from "Pioneers of the Old South," Vol. 5, p. 158, *The Chronicles of America*. Copyright 1918 by Yale University Press.

*The Log College, 1728-1746*

Princeton University. And the Governor was right: they did indeed speak out against what he called the "best" government—it was John Witherspoon, the president of Princeton, who when the bold Declaration of Independence trembled in the balance and might have failed, rose to say:

> For my own part, of property I have some, of reputation more. That reputation is staked, that property is pledged, on the issue of this contest; and although these gray hairs must soon be sent into the Sepulchre, I would infinitely rather that they be sent thither by the hand of the executioner than desert at this crisis the sacred cause of my country.[2]

It is probable that we fail to realize how stern was the test of character put upon the leaders of these early colleges. The log colleges, including some which now occupy places of great power, were not well thought of by the intelligentsia. An early New England geography book says of many of these colleges, "They are not distinguished." And even an evangelical like George

Whitefield declined a Master of Arts degree proffered by the college at Princeton because of the fear of ridicule of his backwoods degree. But difficult as was their task, the colleges did their work well for the Church and for the political and economic life of the country.

In the Southern colonies, William and Mary College was early founded for the education of the Indians. Half a century later the Presbyterian, Samuel Davies, came to preach in Virginia; and his assistant, John Todd, founded an academy in Louisa County. Soon there were many such schools, like Zion Parnassus in North Carolina. Zion Academy at Winnsboro, South Carolina, now long deserted, was so effective that only one Presbyterian college in the South has as many of its alumni in the *Dictionary of American Biography*.

As the Revolution began, Liberty Hall was founded at Lexington, Virginia. The first important gift to this school—a block of stock in the James River Canal Company, worth $50,000—came from George Washington. In recognition of this gift the name of the school was changed to Washington Academy and in 1813 to Washington College. It was originally quite as close to the Presbyterian Church as were colleges like Hampden-Sydney. The great service of Robert E. Lee strengthened it but drew it away from its Presbyterian moorings to its present status as Washington and Lee University, an independent institution with some Presbyterian atmosphere.

Hampden-Sydney College came along in the year of the Revolution. We see the struggle with primitive conditions, as George Craghead wrote:

> The walls of the Academy were about three feet high, and on account of scarcity of room for students to study in, they obtained leave from the undertaker, Mr. Coleman, to erect little huts with the shingles that were intended to cover the Academy. They were packed like a sugar loaf with a plank for three or four boys to sit upon; and in the night a candle being placed in each hut, there being eight or ten, it showed how intent the inhabitants were in studying until nine or ten o'clock at night. That year the students devoted their time to study; very little was spent in recreation or amusement.[3]

Soon after, we read that Hampden-Sydney College had an auditorium, forty by twenty-five feet, and that the main college building was described as "the wonder of the day." Hugh Blair Grigsby says of it: "Travelers would turn aside to see it, and it was undoubtedly the largest brick structure reared by Protestant hands in the cause of education between the falls of James River and the Pacific Ocean."[4]

*Cushing Hall, Hampden-Sydney College*

## After the Revolution: Colleges Prepare for Democracy

This sense of the mutual dependence of piety, learning, and freedom was equally powerful in the time just after the Revolution. The leadership of the Presbyterian Church in this period should not escape notice.

For instance, Transylvania College was founded in Lexington, Kentucky, in 1783. It was affiliated with the Presbyterian Church and had as the original core of its library the books of the Reverend John Todd, son of one of the founders of Hampden-

Sydney. But it gradually left the Presbyterian fold. About the middle of the nineteenth century, the Presbyterian Church was surprised to wake up and find that it had lost all hold on the institution. It is now affiliated with the Disciples of Christ.

The earliest of the state universities were founded in this period, and their founders seem to have had in mind almost exactly the same ends as those of church colleges like Harvard, Yale, and Princeton.

For instance, the University of North Carolina in its early days was so similar in pattern to church colleges that it was constantly criticized as being too close to the Presbyterian Church. The University of Tennessee was founded by William Carrick, pastor of the First Presbyterian Church of Knoxville, Tennessee, and was probably as close to the Church as any of our present church colleges. The same was true of the University of Kentucky. The importance of religion at the University of Georgia in the early days may be gauged by the provision of a fine of two dollars for "laughing at prayers." In all of the institutions dominated by Calvinistic concepts, Christian faith was assumed to be an essential element in education, and it was equally assumed that the program of the Christian Church was dependent upon education.

To Presbyterian pioneers, churches and colleges went together. This spirit is reflected in the life of Samuel Doak, who came from his home in Virginia to East Tennessee. It is recorded of him:

> Doak was riding through a heavily wooded section when he met a party of men felling timber. They found out that he was a preacher and asked him to preach to them. After he had finished, they asked him to stay on with them. Consequently he remained and purchased land. On it he constructed three cabins—one, a home; another, a church; and the third, a school. The school was later chartered in 1784 as Martin's Academy. In 1795 it became Washington College.[5]

Except for Hampden-Sydney, which was founded at the outbreak of the Revolution, we have no Southern Presbyterian college now in existence which traces its lineage back before 1800. But in the period between the Revolution and the end of that century, the Presbyterians were highly active in founding several state universities. Likewise they were instrumental in the founding of Transylvania University (transferred to the Christian Church), Washington College, and Tusculum College (both now connected with the U.S.A. Church).

What was the nature of student life in these waning years of the eighteenth century? Living was harsh and frugal. Cost of room and board at Hampden-Sydney was $9 a year. An English observer says of our American colleges in these early days: "The utmost physical recreation seemed to consist in a country walk, and I doubt if even this was common. This absence of desire for physical sports seems more or less common throughout America, and is very strange in the eyes of those accustomed to the exhibition of animal spirits in the English youth of both sexes."[6]

But life was not wholly given to books. A student in a Presbyterian college in earlier times recorded the following amusements in his diary:

> Strewing the entries in the Night with the greasy Feathers; freezing the Bell; Ringing it at late Hours of the Night . . . writing witty pointed anonymous Papers . . . Picking from the neighborhood now and then a plump fat Hen or Turkey . . . Darting Sunbeams upon the Town-People . . . Making Squibs and other frightful compositions with Gunpowder, & lighting them in the Rooms of timorous Boys and new comers.[7]

Yet in the same college from which this diary came, "the faculty, ever solicitous for the good conduct of the students in their charge, prohibited the game of shinny because it sometimes resulted in accidents and because there were 'many amusements both more honourable and more useful in which they are indulged.'"[8]

These general statements about student life are reflected in the history of our own Presbyterian colleges. At least a part of the constituency of Hampden-Sydney considered the institution too pious. On account of what he regarded as undue interest in religion at the college, Benjamin Harrison withdrew his son, William Henry, from the student body.

On the other hand, we find that Dr. Archibald Alexander, who went to Hampden-Sydney near the close of the eighteenth century, did not share this opinion. Despite his intellectual prowess and personal force, after nine years as the president of Hampden-Sydney and "weary of wrestling with the control of young men," he returned to the pastorate. Incidentally, we read that disciplinary problems at Princeton about this time were very similar.

## Before "The War": Era of Expansion

Before the War Between the States, the South occupied a position of high influence in the nation. Men like Basil Manly, a Baptist minister and president of the University of Alabama, and a Presbyterian, J. H. Thornwell, president of the College of South Carolina, were among the chief intellectual powers in the United States.

In education, the South was making heroic efforts.

Twice as many young men per thousand of the population were in colleges in the lower South or in some of the Eastern institutions as were sent from similar groups in other parts of the country. Eleven thousand students were enrolled in the colleges of the cotton states, while in Massachusetts, with half as many white people as were found in all the cotton states, there were only 1733 college students. Illinois, with a population of 1,712,000 or more than half as many white people, had three thousand young men in her colleges. The income of all the higher institutions of the lower South in 1860 was $708,000, which represented an increase of more than a hundred per cent over the figures for 1850. The six New England states, with the best public school system in the world outside of Germany and with an accumulated wealth far in excess of that of the cotton region, spent only $368,469 per year in collegiate education, and their population of 3,235,000 sent only 3,748 young men to college.[9]

This was one of the great sacrificial periods in the history of Presbyterian education in the United States. As we learn of the poverty that hounded these men at Tusculum; as we read of the physical and mental breakdown of Isaac Anderson, who had struggled to carry Maryville for so many years; as we see Archibald Alexander struggle for nine years at Hampden-Sydney College; as we see the great preacher Daniel Baker and his travels for the raising of funds for Austin College, we are bound to ask, "Why was all this done?" The answer is plain: these men believed that if the Church is to enlighten the people, there must be an *educated* ministry, and if our lay leaders are to rise to high power in the service of God, they too must be educated. And they were willing to put into this whatever toil, tears, and blood might be necessary.

This dedication to the cause of an educated ministry resulted in the Cumberland controversy. A large segment of the Church in the West demanded the lessening of education requirements for the ministry. The leaders of the Presbyterian Church held firm even as the dissenting brethren withdrew to form the Cumberland Presbyterian Church. The chief thing to note is not the decision, but the ideal that stood behind it: that education was the essence of the program of the Presbyterian Church, never to be given up under any circumstances.

In this period the first important educational activity in the Presbyterian Church was the founding of Union Theological Seminary. Dr. Moses Hoge began his divinity classes in 1807. As his work was sanctioned by the Synod of Virginia in 1812, the latter is taken as the date of the founding of the Seminary, which was located at Hampden-Sydney College until 1898, and then moved to Richmond, Virginia.

Centre College was founded in 1819, the second in age of the colleges now connected with Southern Presbyterianism. Originally independent, it came under the control of the Church in 1824. In 1853 what is now the Louisville Presbyterian Seminary began its service in Danville, along with Centre College.

In 1828 Columbia Theological Seminary was founded at Lexington, Georgia. It was removed to Columbia, South Carolina, in 1830. We are indebted to it for training Dr. B. M. Palmer and Dr. J. H. Thornwell, who shaped so much of the thought and life of the Southern Presbyterian Church, and Dr. John Leighton Wilson, who did so much to mold its missionary spirit.

Davidson College, the largest of Southern Presbyterian educational institutions, was founded in 1837. After twenty years of bitter struggle, the college was firmly established by a munificent gift from Mr. Maxwell Chambers of Salisbury, not a member of the Presbyterian Church. The War Between the States destroyed much of its endowment but the college struggled through to 1900. After that, it began to grow.

In 1842, Dr. Rufus W. Bailey came to Staunton, Virginia, to found what is now one of the oldest institutions of higher learning for women. At first called Augusta Female Seminary, it is now Mary Baldwin College. Miss Mary Julia Baldwin became principal in 1863—a time which called for unusual courage and resourcefulness to keep any school open in the Shenandoah Valley, then a battlefield for the armies of the Union and the Confederacy. During Miss Baldwin's long administration (1863-1897) the quality of courses was gradually raised in most departments to the equivalent of college work. Throughout its history, the college has been associated with the Presbyterian Church.

In these same years, Austin College opened its doors in Huntsville, Texas. The father of the college was the flaming evangelist Daniel Baker. He was at once its local administrator and its ambassador to all the Presbyterian world. He preached over a very wide territory, always raising funds for Austin College. Dr. Baker's success in fund-raising was so great that one observer remarked: "Possibly more people from all parts of the nation have small investments in Austin College than in any other college in America."

Keeping the doors of Austin College open, however, required constant and continued effort; and sometimes results were disheartening. One of the early presidents records that on one of his trips he traveled more than 400 miles on horseback through eastern Texas to raise money for the college, but collected not one cent for the college indebtedness and only $5 to pay expenses of his trip. Of another occasion he writes:

> I came to a swollen stream after a heavy rain. I swam my horse across, but drifted so far down stream that the bank was too steep for my horse to take me up. I threw my overcoat and saddle-bags on the bank, got off in the water and was leading my horse up the bank when he slipped, jerked the bridle rein from my hand and swam to the other side of the stream. Not being able to swim, I hung my baggage on a tree, rolled a log on the bank into the water, got a pole with which I could touch bottom, mounted the log, and started for my horse. The log kept turning and I got ducked first on this side and then on that, but finally got over alive. I caught my horse

and rode well up stream before swimming across; thus struck the bank at the right place. A 'norther' was blowing and I was nearly frozen.[10]

Southwestern at Memphis began its service in 1848, in Clarksville, Tennessee, under the title of Montgomery Masonic College. In 1855 the Synod of Nashville assumed control of the college, naming it for its new president, Dr. W. M. Stewart. In 1875, under the the administration of Dr. J. B. Shearer, it was incorporated as Southwestern Presbyterian University, when a theological department of instruction was added.

## Two Seminaries United at Louisville

In 1853, the Theological Seminary of the Presbyterian Church, U.S.A. was founded at Danville, Kentucky. The Louisville Theological Seminary of the Presbyterian Church, U. S. was founded in 1893. The two were united at Louisville in 1901 as the Presbyterian Theological Seminary of Kentucky, and in May 1927, the Board of Directors changed the name to the Louisville Presbyterian Theological Seminary.

In Missouri, Westminster College was founded in 1851, as Fulton College. It was chartered as Westminster College in 1853. It was the only Protestant college exclusively for men west of the Mississippi.

Many other ambitious educational projects of the Church were begun in this period. The Female College of Concord Presbytery began its work in Statesville, North Carolina, with high hopes. An advertisement in the *Western Democrat* stated that the term was to be five months, and that the total expenses to the student were $98.50, "with candles and towels furnished by the pupils." This institution began in such fashion as to promise the very highest of success, but it never fully recovered from the crushing blow of 1861-1865.

Peace College was another of these educational enterprises of the Church, begun in 1857, prospering until the War Between the States. In the same period, Queens College was founded in Charlotte, as Charlotte Female Institute.

Presbyterians ought to know that these colleges made a genuine contribution to the intellectual life of their times. For example, beginning about 1836 Dr. John William Draper conducted at Hampden-Sydney numerous experiments in the study of light. In connection with these he made a camera remarkably similar to instruments now in use, and capable of making pictures of a quality comparable to modern photography. "Although Daguerre is credited with achieving the first practical photography, the time of exposure required with his method was so long that portraits were impossible. By experimenting with silver bromide, Dr. Draper was able to cut down on exposure time and make portraiture practical. The first complete portrait of a person ever recorded with normal light was made by Dr. Draper."[11]

As this period closed with the War Between the States, we catch this glimpse of students going to war:

> Trains were passing loaded with troops from Virginia and other parts of the South, bands played "Dixie," the "Marseillaise," and other inspiring strains. While we waited the boys were busy leaving souvenirs, tokens, etc., and the girls were scratching names on canteens, tin cups, and pewter spoons. As we heard the whistle of our train, the girls en masse gathered around Captain Atkinson and were showering kisses on him. A lieutenant looked on awhile until his "best girl" approached, when he offered to relieve Captain Atkinson of this part of his arduous duties. "I can stand the firing yet, lieutenant," replied the captain; "if it becomes too heavy, I'll call on you."[12]

## The Late Nineteenth Century: Era of Stabilization

In the period after the War Between the States, Southern Presbyterians, though prostrated by war, were still building colleges, still believing that this was an essential part of their service to the world.

The war had destroyed much of the educational program of the Presbyterian Church. Many of the colleges were closed, all of them lost much of their endowments, and many lost part of their buildings. In one case, the president of a college died of smallpox contracted in nursing soldiers who had just put him out of his house and destroyed everything that could be burned in the college buildings. In 1865, Southern Presbyterians approached the task of rebuilding their shattered educational work.

In 1866 the Reverend James King and his friend, Dr. George A. Caldwell, pastor of the First Presbyterian Church in Bristol, Tennessee, began the bold venture of establishing a college upon the still-smoking embers of the great conflagration. Mr. King died just before the first classes were held, but King College bears his name.

The college was for many years kept alive chiefly by the sacrificial gifts and labors of two Bristol laymen, E. W. King and James D. Faucette. In spite of poverty its early years must have been characterized by remarkable academic soundness. An unusually high percentage of its alumni entered the Presbyterian ministry. There was one ten-year period in which four alumni of King College were elected Moderators of the General Assembly of the U. S. Church, while another from the same group became Moderator of the U.S.A. General Assembly.

Arkansas College began its service in 1872. The college had a very hard struggle until about 1900 when a period of improvement began.

One of the most interesting of Presbyterian educational institutions is Stillman College, founded in 1873 as a junior college and theological seminary for Negro men. Later it was made coeducational. It is sustained and governed by the General Assembly's Board of Church Extension.

Among the alumni of Stillman College was the Reverend William H. Sheppard, D.D., whom Dr. S. H. Chester of the Board of World Missions introduced on one occasion with these words:

> It is my privilege to introduce to you today perhaps the most distinguished and certainly the most widely known minister of our Southern Presbyterian Church. For one thing, he is the only minister on our roll holding a fellowship in the Royal Geographical Society of London. . . . During the time of his missionary service he has been called to represent us on many important occasions. He has stood before kings as our representative. . . . He is now recognized both in London and in Brussels as one of the greatest of African missionaries.[13]

The Presbyterians of South Carolina founded their college in

1872. Dr. Jacobs writes: ". . . our people publicly met in a store in . . . 1872, and doggedly set to work to organize this High School Association, raising funds to repair the building. It was from this little start that in 1880 developed the Presbyterian College of South Carolina."[14]

The institution was known as Clinton College, 1880-1890; Presbyterian College of South Carolina, 1890-1928; and Presbyterian College after 1928 when the Synods of Georgia and South Carolina assumed joint ownership and control.

The Presbyterian apostle of the Kentucky mountains was Dr. Edward O. Guerrant. He labored in the center of a territory whose long isolation from church influences and the church's educational program contributed to its uncomplimentary nickname of that period, "Bloody Breathitt." One of the chief factors in the great program of Dr. Guerrant and his "Soul-winners' Society" was Lees College. The year was 1883; and the town was Jackson.

In 1889, in Decatur, Georgia, a very different program was begun. At that time Dr. Frank H. Gaines, and his elders in the Decatur Presbyterian Church, began an institution known first as Decatur Female Seminary. The name was changed to Agnes Scott Institute and later to Agnes Scott College in memory of the mother of Col. George W. Scott, who gave the new school its first building.

Under the leadership of Miss Nannette Hopkins, the first principal, a high spiritual note characterized the very beginning of this college. In its early days its leaders entered into a solemn covenant to pray daily for each other in the work in the college, for each student, and for the baptism of the college in the Holy Spirit so that it might become a fountain of blessing.

The educational history of the Synod of Mississippi presents graphically what has taken place repeatedly in our denomination: Church leaders have too often founded colleges in response to their hearts, without securing resources for the sustenance of these institutions. Many times this has resulted in a long and heroic struggle, characterized by great sacrifice on the part of a few individuals, finally ending in the closing of an institution.

Thus, for many years the Presbyterians of Mississippi scattered their efforts in the education of women among several institutions. There was Chickasaw Female College, founded at Pontotoc, Mississippi, in 1862. There was Mississippi Synodical College at Holly Springs, founded in 1883. There was McComb Female Institute; there was Central Mississippi Institute. None of these is now operating in its original form. Most of them have been merged with Belhaven College, which was not originally a Presbyterian institution.

Flora Macdonald College is the successor to Floral College, which served "the Scottish Center of America" from 1841 to 1878, and which was the first institution in North Carolina to grant diplomas to women. Red Springs College was founded in the same neighborhood in 1896. In 1915 the Scottish Society of America, under the leadership of Dr. James A. Macdonald, distinguished editor of the *Toronto Globe*, asked that the name of Flora Macdonald be attached to the college to commemorate the daring Scottish lassie who rescued "Bonnie Prince Charlie" in 1746.

President Walter W. Moore of Union Theological Seminary once declared that no man who had gone out from that Seminary had done more for the Kingdom of God than had Edgar Tufts. The Banner Elk Presbyterian Church, Grace Hospital, Grandfather Orphanage, and Lees-McRae College are institutional evidence of his work in the North Carolina mountains. The college developed from a small summer mission school. In 1899 Dr. Tufts "gathered around an open fire in his own room fewer than a dozen of the most advanced pupils, and for a few months endeavored to stimulate their minds to higher ideals in life." The next autumn a school was founded with gifts of $250 in cash and lumber, subscribed at a prayer meeting in the Banner Elk Church. This early school, and the present college, have retained a very practical tone: nursing and homemaking arts have occupied a large place in the educational program.

As the nineteenth century came to a close, the Presbyterian Church seemed still to believe in education, and was still building colleges. It had not, up to that time, created any institution which could be called well-established, but there was no dramatic evidence of waning interest on the part of the Church.

## Twentieth-Century Efforts: First 40 Years

The short space of this chapter will not permit mention of the many developments among our institutions during this century. Each reader is urged to acquaint himself fully with the Presbyterian institutions which serve his area. A card to the Registrar of any of the colleges will bring informative literature. We shall briefly record the new institutions which came into being from 1900 to 1940.

The Austin Presbyterian Theological Seminary was founded in 1902 by the Synod of Texas. In 1906 the Synod of Arkansas joined in the support of the Seminary, followed by Oklahoma in 1910 and Louisiana in 1929.

In 1904 Senator Henry G. Davis joined his son-in-law, Senator Steven B. Elkins, in the founding of Davis and Elkins College, under the care of Lexington Presbytery. Later Mrs. Elkins gave her handsome estate, Halliehurst, as the new site of the school. In 1908 the Synod of West Virginia, U.S.A., joined in the control of the college.

In 1914 the General Assembly's Training School for Lay Workers was founded in Richmond in rented buildings. In 1922 the present handsome campus on Brook Road in Richmond was acquired.

In 1916 Dr. R. C. Anderson began to conduct in the buildings of the Mountain Retreat Association a normal school for girls, with the chief emphasis upon training them as public school teachers. Gradually this grew into a junior college and then into the present four-year institution, Montreat College.

In 1914, Captain Charles Schreiner, who had left his home in Alsace at the age of fourteen, and had large success in business in Texas, announced his intention to establish a junior college and preparatory school for boys at Kerrville. World War I interrupted these plans, but in 1917 Captain Schreiner placed in trust 140 acres of land and $250,000 to be conveyed to the Synod of Texas after the cessation of war. Captain Schreiner expressed the hope that the institution would be conducted as a military school. On December 27, 1921, the Synod received the trust and began erecting the building for the school, Schreiner Institute.

In 1925 the Theological Department at Southwestern Theological University was discontinued. The college was moved to its present imposing campus in Memphis, Tennessee, and its name was changed to its present form, Southwestern at Memphis. This move, one of the boldest in our educational history, left the college at one time more than $725,000 in debt. But the faith and courage of President Charles E. Diehl and his trustees would not be denied. The debt was paid in 1930, and when Dr. Diehl retired in 1949 he left an endowment of almost $3,000,000.

In this period, the Appalachia Synod was formed and immediately took responsibility for King College. In 1931 the closing of Stonewall Jackson College was followed by the admission of women students to King College.

In 1928, the Synod of North Carolina purchased the property of Carolina College, a Methodist institution established in Maxton in 1911. Immediately the Presbyterian Junior College for Men was established at Maxton, and it has continued in operation since that time.

The remarkable growth of Davidson College from 300 students in 1910 to 675 by 1930 and 852 in 1955 has been accompanied by great physical expansion. This was aided by a gift of about $1,800,-000 made in 1924 by James B. Duke, who was not a Presbyterian.

Arkansas College, after a period of depression, gained strength through a financial campaign that added more than $200,000 to its endowment. Buildings are being erected on a new campus near the edge of the city, and another and larger financial campaign is getting under way.

What were the accomplishments of Southern Presbyterians in higher education between 1900 and 1940? Compared with the sacrificial and persistent efforts of Presbyterians of other centuries, much seems to be lacking. Presbyterian colleges, with a few fine exceptions, were complacent about seeking admission to accrediting associations. Gifts to education in other church groups far exceeded those in Presbyterian circles. In fact, during the first forty years of the century, a Methodist layman gave to one Methodist college a gift that was, at the time, four times the equivalent of all the endowment and all the buildings of all Southern Presbyterian institutions.

Presbyterians were not behind other groups in contributions to missions or church buildings or local church work; but their support of higher education lagged sorely during these four decades.

## Conclusion: An Evaluation and a Challenge

As one glances back across this long history, he finds some room for encouragement, some room for elation. At some points he is moved to stand with his head bowed in solemn thankfulness to God for the heroic efforts of the saints of other times.

And he is bound to be grateful for the signs of some fundamental improvements in the situation in recent years: the Church undoubtedly has made better efforts since 1940 than at any other period in the twentieth century. In recent years significant financial campaigns have been conducted at Presbyterian College at Clinton, South Carolina, and at Hampden-Sydney. Austin College has been greatly developed by a financial campaign and by the munificent gifts of Mr. M. B. Hughey. Arkansas College has in a few years been brought from a position approaching abject hopelessness to a very encouraging situation. There is prospect that the Synod of North Carolina may do the almost unique thing of uniting several struggling units into a highly influential institution, instead of waiting to lose some or all of them in the dismal fashion so common in the past.

This is gratifying progress. But any observer is bound to see some other stern facts: In 1914, Dr. Henry H. Sweets issued for the Executive Committee of Christian Education a book entitled *Our Presbyterian Educational Institutions 1913-1914*. In this volume appear the names of fifteen colleges which are now defunct. The Church has in this generation lost more colleges than in any other period of her history. And neutral observers are telling us that the remaining colleges are now in greater danger than ever before. Unwise plans, or the indifferent following of good plans, can lead to further loss of influence. The Church should understand and act upon this stern warning. The next chapter will discuss more completely the church college today.

## THROUGH THE YEARS

Many Presbyterian colleges were founded which served their purposes well. Then, when the need for them had passed, they quietly closed their doors. Many others, however, have continued to serve through the years. The Presbyterian (U.S.) colleges which are active today are listed below, in the order of their founding:

### Early Years

| | |
|---|---|
| 1776 | Hampden-Sydney |

### Nineteenth Century: First Period

| | |
|---|---|
| 1812 | Union Theological Seminary |
| 1819 | Centre College* |
| 1828 | Columbia Theological Seminary |
| 1836 | Davidson College |
| 1842 | Mary Baldwin College |
| 1849 | Austin College |
| 1853 | Westminster College* |
| 1856 | Mitchell College |
| 1857 | Queens College |
| 1857 | Peace College |

### Nineteenth Century: Last Period

| | |
|---|---|
| 1869 | King College |
| 1872 | Arkansas College |
| 1875 | Southwestern |
| 1876 | Stillman College |
| 1880 | Presbyterian College |
| 1889 | Agnes Scott College |
| 1890 | Lees Junior College |
| 1893 | Belhaven College |
| 1896 | Flora Macdonald College |

### Twentieth Century

| | |
|---|---|
| 1900 | Lees-McRae College |
| 1901 | Louisville Theological Seminary* |
| 1902 | Austin Theological Seminary |
| 1904 | Davis and Elkins* |
| 1914 | Assembly's Training School |
| 1916 | Montreat College |
| 1923 | Schreiner Institute |
| 1929 | Presbyterian Junior College |

---

* Jointly owned and controlled with the Presbyterian Church in the United States of America.

## PRESBYTERIAN INSTITUTIONS OF HIGHER LEARNING, RESOURCES, 1940-1955
### (in thousands of dollars)

| SENIOR COLLEGES | Value of Property | | Endowment | | Total Resources | | Increase in Resources |
|---|---|---|---|---|---|---|---|
| | 1940 ($1,000's) | 1955 ($1,000's) | 1940 ($1,000's) | 1955 ($1,000's) | 1940 ($1,000's) | 1955 ($1,000's) | 1940-1955 ($1,000's) |
| Agnes Scott* . . . . | 1,912 | 4,400 | 1,687 | 3,200 | 3,599 | 7,600 | 4,001 |
| Arkansas . . . . | 373 | 732 | 65 | 330 | 438 | 1,062 | 624 |
| Austin . . . . | 700 | 2,156 | 260 | 1,110 | 960 | 3,266 | 2,306 |
| Belhaven . . . . | 762 | 770 | 80 | 665 | 842 | 1,435 | 593 |
| Centre . . . . | 913 | 1,626 | 1,336 | 2,604 | 2,249 | 4,230 | 1,981 |
| Davidson . . . . | 1,500 | 4,652 | 3,000† | 7,246 | 4,500 | 11,898 | 7,398 |
| Davis and Elkins . . | 550 | 1,600 | 185 | 274 | 736 | 1,874 | 1,138 |
| Flora Macdonald . . | 286 | 390 | 161 | 422 | 447 | 813 | 366 |
| Hampden-Sydney . | 673 | 1,086 | 372 | 1,318 | 1,045 | 2,404 | 1,360 |
| King . . . . | 300 | 590 | 137 | 815 | 437 | 1,405 | 968 |
| Mary Baldwin* . . | 693 | 1,344 | 521 | 611 | 1,213 | 1,955 | 741 |
| Montreat . . . . | 100 | 234 | 3 | 276 | 103 | 510 | 407 |
| Presbyterian . . . | 792 | 1,075 | 80 | 629 | 871 | 1,704 | 833 |
| Queens . . . . | 733 | 2,030 | 313 | 674 | 1,046 | 2,704 | 1,658 |
| Southwestern (Memphis) | 1,509 | 4,092 | 454 | 2,825 | 1,963 | 6,917 | 4,954 |
| Stillman . . . . | 323 | 976 | 100 | 456 | 423 | 1,432 | 1,009 |
| Westminster . . . | 608 | 934 | 845 | 604 | 1,454 | 1,538 | 84 |
| TOTALS . . . . | 12,727 | 28,687 | 9,599 | 24,059 | 22,326 | 52,747 | 30,421 |

*affiliated
†adjusted

|  | | | | | | | |
|---|---|---|---|---|---|---|---|
| **JUNIOR COLLEGES** | | | | | | | |
| Lees Junior . . . . . | 181 | 325 | 2 | 140 | 183 | 465 | 282 |
| Lees-McRae . . . . | 388 | 605 | 117 | 387 | 505 | 992 | 487 |
| Mitchell . . . . . | 150 | 288 | 10 | 38 | 160 | 327 | 167 |
| Peace . . . . . | 350 | 500 | 12 | 225 | 362 | 725 | 363 |
| Presbyterian Junior . . | 170 | 279 | 18 | 315 | 188 | 594 | 406 |
| Schreiner . . . . | 678 | 1,125 | 175 | 250 | 853 | 1,375 | 522 |
| TOTALS . . . . . | 1,917 | 3,122 | 334 | 1,355 | 2,251 | 4,478 | 2,227 |
| **SEMINARIES AND TRAINING SCHOOL** | | | | | | | |
| Austin . . . . . | 125 | 772 | 350 | 1,229 | 475 | 2,001 | 1,526 |
| Columbia . . . . | 500 | 1,367 | 370 | 1,085 | 870 | 2,452 | 1,582 |
| Louisville . . . . | 442 | 654 | 1,023 | 1,833 | 1,465 | 2,487 | 1,022 |
| Union . . . . . | 753 | 1,623 | 1,040 | 3,829 | 1,793 | 5,452 | 3,659 |
| Assembly's Training School | 591 | 947 | 135 | 1,044 | 726 | 1,991 | 1,265 |
| TOTALS . . . . . | 2,411 | 5,363 | 2,918 | 9,020 | 5,329 | 14,383 | 9,054 |
| GRAND TOTAL . . . | 17,055 | 37,172 | 12,851 | 34,434 | 29,906 | 71,608 | 41,702 |

SOURCE: *Minutes, Presbyterian Educational Association of the South, 1940 and 1955*

## JOHN ROOD CUNNINGHAM

President, Davidson College, 1941—.

A.B., Westminster College, Fulton, Mo., 1914; B.D., Louisville Presbyterian Theological Seminary, 1917; D.D., Westminster College, 1925. Given LL.D. degrees by King College, Duke University, Wake Forest College, and University of North Carolina.

Pastorates at Grenada, Miss.; Gainesville, Fla.; Bristol, Va.; and Winston-Salem, N. C.

President, Louisville Presbyterian Seminary, 1930-36.

Member of Board, Union Theological Seminary, Richmond, Va.

Moderator, Presbyterian Church (U.S.) General Assembly, 1947-48.

President, Association of American Colleges, 1952-53.

Has served on many interdenominational and international committees of the Church.

# What Is a Christian College?

## ITS CONTRIBUTION AND SIGNIFICANCE

## *John R. Cunningham*

### The Church College's Strategic Functions

IN THE SUMMER of 1955 President Gordon Gray of the University of North Carolina delivered the Charter Day address at the University of California in Los Angeles. President Gray said:

> However, even as president of the oldest state university in America, I would have to say that if I were presented with a choice between a system of private higher education and a system of public higher education, I would select the former. Fortunately, no such alternative is presented. Indeed, my concern is that we do all we can to avoid having the other choice thrust upon us by circumstances.[1]

These are significant words coming from the president of a state university. They should remind us of a basic educational responsibility of the Church.

Are we Presbyterians really awake to the vast contributions of our church colleges to Church and nation? Are we convinced that they have a significant place in the future as well? We have noted in earlier chapters that these Presbyterian colleges came into being through the convictions and the sacrifices of their founders. Only if we cherish that same concern will we retain the church colleges and their benefits to our generation.

Education upon a Christian basis is central, not peripheral, in the life of our nation and of the Church. True, evangelism is the first task of the Church, but that task is not finished until those who acknowledge Christ as Saviour are taught and matured in the meaning of Christian faith and character. Otherwise the Church is loaded with "babes" who are neither mature nor serviceable. There must be growth in Christian character, insight, purpose, power, if there is to be an adequate, intelligent leadership for the winning of the world to Christ. Likewise, as a young person's knowledge of the material world around him enlarges through education, so too should his knowledge and understanding of spiritual values expand and deepen. These two functions merge in the total program of the church college.

## Education Is Big Business

When we think of education in the United States we are thinking about big business. We are people with a passion for education. In proportion to population, more than five times as many young people go to college here as in England; seven times as many as in Germany; ten times as many as in France; and twenty times as many as in India. So rapid has been the growth of education in our nation that we have come to take higher education for granted, but let's look at the figures:

1850.......... 116 colleges............   11,900 stduents
1900.......... 485 colleges............ 238,000 students
1950..........1,700 colleges............2,350,000 students
1970.......... ?   ........estimated 4,500,000 students

In less than fifteen years from now, the college population is expected to be double what it was in 1950. An unprecedented problem faces us on all levels in American education: the problem of caring for the rising tide of enrollment, beginning at the first grade and going through college and university levels. We can now foresee with considerable certainty that by 1960 our college enrollment will have increased to 3,000,000 and then will rise to the 4,500,000 mark, as indicated.

How much of this increase will become the burden of church

# AMERICA'S DUAL SYSTEM OF HIGHER EDUCATION

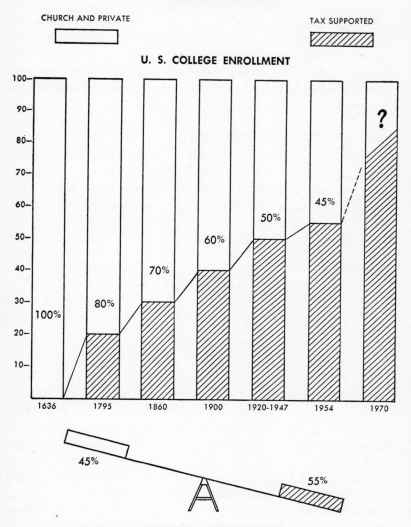

CHURCH AND PRIVATE

TAX SUPPORTED

## U. S. COLLEGE ENROLLMENT

How far should the balance swing?

schools? Until recently the majority of our college and university students were in church-related and other private colleges and universities. Within the last few decades the balance has changed so that now the greater number are in tax-supported institutions. But even with the increased enrollment in state-supported colleges, a significantly large proportion of our young people still seek their education in church colleges. Certainly these church colleges must be prepared to handle an increasing number of the young folk who will seek higher education.

## What Are Our Presbyterian Colleges?

At the outset it is important that we know what are the institutions supported by our Church. These include four theological seminaries, the General Assembly's Training School for Lay Workers, seventeen four-year colleges, and six junior colleges. (See list on page 76.) Total enrollment for 1955 was 9,030, broken down into categories as follows:

| | |
|---|---|
| Senior Colleges | 6,739 |
| Junior Colleges | 1,412 |
| Seminaries | 750 |
| Assembly's Training School | 129 |

Actually, the Church finances only a minor part of the total cost of operation of these colleges. For example, tabulation of costs in eight of the larger colleges in a recent year showed that 12.33 per cent was paid from the benevolence funds of the Church. Student fees accounted for 55.72 per cent, endowment income 25.77 per cent, and other gifts 6.18 per cent. However, most of the colleges need this financial support from the Church to keep alive.

How does the Church exercise authority over the church college? This relationship may take a variety of forms.

Some colleges are legally owned and controlled by a church court, such as the synod, in the Presbyterian system of government. The trustees under such condition are elected by the synod and administer the college for and in the name of the synod.

*Location of Presbyterian Colleges and Seminaries*

On the other hand, the relationship with the Church may be less definite. The college may historically owe its origin to the influence of the Church, but may have acquired property in its own right. The synod, if the college were church-related, would elect some of the trustees, but different provisions might be made for others. The final authority in this instance would probably be the board of trustees. The college would continue to associate itself with other institutions of the same denomination, and to receive information, advice, and help from the denomination.

Between these two extremes of all-out ownership and control on one hand, and a rather loose church-relatedness on the other, are a wide variety of forms of control, with each college charter legally defining regulations for organization and operation.

The Presbyterian Church in the United States historically has located the control and support of its institutions of higher education at the synod level. This localizing of control and support has apparently been wise, as is seen when comparisons are made with denominations which have placed support and control at the national level. When church members are close to the institutions which look to them for support, there is a more personal understanding of college or seminary needs and opportunities.

## PRESBYTERIAN (U.S.) INSTITUTIONS OF HIGHER EDUCATION

| Name | Location | 1955 Enrollment | From the Church |
|---|---|---|---|
| **SENIOR COLLEGES** | | | |
| Agnes Scott | Decatur, Georgia | 537 | $ –0– |
| Arkansas | Batesville, Arkansas | 178 | 45,000.00 |
| Austin | Sherman, Texas | 611 | 43,500.00 |
| Belhaven | Jackson, Mississippi | 161 | 26,102.20 |
| *Centre | Danville, Kentucky | 403 | 29,468.34 |
| Davidson | Davidson, North Carolina | 852 | 23,066.00 |
| *Davis and Elkins | Elkins, West Virginia | 499 | 57,394.70 |
| Flora Macdonald | Red Springs, North Carolina | 288 | 19,560.00 |
| Hampden-Sydney | Hampden-Sydney, Virginia | 353 | 20,532.00 |
| King | Bristol, Tennessee | 225 | 52,076.86 |
| Mary Baldwin | Staunton, Virginia | 255 | 10,501.50 |
| Montreat | Montreat, North Carolina | 212 | 17,489.00 |
| Presbyterian | Clinton, South Carolina | 511 | 62,882.00 |
| Queens | Charlotte, North Carolina | 434 | 30,491.14 |
| Southwestern | Memphis, Tennessee | 569 | 99,926.84 |
| Stillman | Tuscaloosa, Alabama | 308 | 73,760.51 |
| *Westminster | Fulton, Missouri | 343 | 29,805.78 |
| **JUNIOR COLLEGES** | | | |
| Lees Junior | Jackson, Kentucky | 323 | 12,295.99 |
| Lees-McRae | Banner Elk, North Carolina | 293 | 8,000.00 |
| Mitchell | Statesville, North Carolina | 161 | 20,880.50 |
| Peace | Raleigh, North Carolina | 255 | 12,577.77 |
| Presbyterian Junior | Maxton, North Carolina | 198 | 10,504.00 |
| Schreiner Institute | Kerrville, Texas | 182 | 9,458.33 |
| **SEMINARIES** | | | |
| Austin Presbyterian Theological | Austin, Texas | 142 | $61,788.00 |
| Columbia Theological | Decatur, Georgia | 205 | 52,605.27 |
| *Louisville Presbyterian Theological | Louisville, Kentucky | 143 | 71,946.97 |
| Union Theological | Richmond, Virginia | 260 | 49,642.00 |
| **TRAINING SCHOOL** | | | |
| Assembly's Training School | Richmond, Virginia | 129 | 122,420.70 |

But this synodical support and control should never be taken to mean that only the controlling synod is interested in the welfare of an institution. Each college, seminary, and Westminster Fellowship serves the entire Church. A church in Texas may draw its minister from Union Seminary in Virginia, and a Virginia church may have as its pastor a graduate of Austin Theological Seminary. Davidson College in North Carolina will enroll students from Tennessee, and North Carolina boys will be in the student body at Southwestern. The effectiveness of the Campus Christian Life program at the University of Florida is a concern of all Presbyterians, for the graduate of any one university or college may be residing anywhere in the United States or abroad. Our Church has an interest in all the institutions of higher education within its territory; although for practical means of operation and support the work of higher education is vested in synods.

## Contributions of Presbyterian Colleges

It can be said without hesitation that the Church has been the mother of education in this country. Of the first 118 colleges east of the Mississippi, 104 were established by the Church. In existence today are 182 colleges and universities founded prior to 1860; 180 of these were organized under the influence of the Church. Presbyterians took the lead in the establishment of 49, Methodists 34, Baptists 25, Congregationalists 21, Roman Catholics 14, Episcopalians 11, other denominations 26. Our founding fathers believed in the principles of Christian education. They manifested considerable genius in putting their faith to work. They looked upon Christian education as a guarantee of self-preservation for the Church. Without the colleges they saw the Church endangered and lacking in those qualities of leadership and character which are essential to our nation's life. Most of the ministers were then, and are now, provided by the church college; and not only so, but the lay leaders of the Church—her teachers, her missionaries, and her other workers—come in large measure from her own institutions.

The Presbyterian Church, early in our nation's history, identified itself in a special way with education. It insisted upon an educated ministry. Near the Presbyterian church there usually stood the school; and not infrequently the minister was also the teacher. The word "parson" was derived from the word "person," as he was called originally because of his superior education and leadership.

---

## WHAT COLLEGES DO OUR MINISTERS COME FROM?

We have now\* 1,049 ministerial candidates, of whom 1,006 are known to have attended some college. Some have attended both tax-supported and church colleges, but many have attended only church colleges. A few have not yet attended college.

*Of 432 candidates now in theological seminaries:*
Attended church-related colleges.................. 225
Attended tax-supported or independent........... 111
Attended both kinds............................. 89
Attended no college............................. 10

*Of 357 candidates now in colleges:*
Attended church-related colleges.................. 250
Attended tax-supported or independent........... 68
Attended both kinds............................. 39

*Of the 260 ministerial candidates who are not now in either seminary or college (in armed services, working, still in high school, location unknown):*
Attended church-related colleges.................. 121
Attended tax-supported or independent........... 60
Both kinds...................................... 46
No college or don't know....................... 33

---

\* Figures as of December, 1954.

---

These small institutions, thus inspired, permitted the impact of strong, cultured, well-educated personalities upon generations of young men who in turn became the leaders in our nation's early history. In a material way, the increasing number of college graduates has contributed to greater productive power within the nation. Since church colleges have educated many of these men they have had a share in this productive capacity.

Particularly, the church college may justly be said to furnish a considerable majority of church leadership. A Davidson College statement recently showed that one half of the Presbyterian ministers in North Carolina, and approximately one fourth of those in the General Assembly, are her alumni. Other church colleges have likewise proved training grounds for church leaders.

The story is not told, however, when we refer to ordained leadership. Among the laity of the Church a disproportionate number of the devoted and intelligent leaders are found to be products of the church colleges. The late William Allen White, a great editor, held that the Church's future rested squarely upon its ability to produce an able, constructive leadership. He stated:

> If Christianity is to survive it must survive in the environment made by Christian leaders. . . . Unless those who believe in a Christian civilization are willing to sacrifice their good, hard-earned cash to educate Christian leaders, they will find in a few generations that their dream has vanished. . . . If the American churchmen fail to support the kind of colleges that turn out Christian leaders, American life under another leadership soon will close the churches.[2]

Furthermore, the church college has set a standard in quality for education, both private and public. Not infrequently our leaders in tax-supported institutions refer to the dependence they feel upon the private liberal arts colleges, including church colleges, in setting the pace for education. In most of these institutions there is freedom for experimentation. There is the privilege of selecting the student body, and the opportunity for infusing Christian character into the whole process. Within the last few years there has been a veritable chorus of expressions from the great industries in America indicating their confidence in these independent church-related colleges and showing their desire to employ their graduates for places of responsibility and leadership.

Dr. William M. Compton, in emphasizing the value of a liberal education, has said:

> The answer to our problem is not in the adventures of science, important as these may be, nor in engineering formulae, nor in spectacular inventions, nor in the marvels of technology, but in the minds and hearts and consciences of men and women. A stream

rises no higher than its source. The ethics of a nation in its public and private affairs and in its international relations are no higher than the ethics of its people. We need public confidence; and we need institutions which can preserve it without pulling the shades down. Righteousness does not come by statute or edict or treaty. It is a matter of the spirit. Only religion can inspire it. Only education can foster and sustain it. This is the endless challenge to liberal education.[3]

The president of my alma mater, Westminster College in Missouri, was recently in New York in conference with five of his alumni. Here he was in our greatest city conferring with the graduates of a small Presbyterian college in the Midwest; yet who were these five men? One was the vice-president of the Bell Laboratories; another was the vice-president of the Worthington Pump Corporation; a third was the vice-president of Union Carbon and Carbide; the fourth was the vice-president in charge of research of the same company; a fifth was the assistant vice-president of American Telephone and Telegraph.

And finally, the church college is constantly making its broad, deep impact upon the strength of our nation as a whole. A recent survey of the Presbyterian colleges of North Carolina contains this statement:

> The church-related college fills an extremely influential position in a world which is hungry for life's highest spiritual values. It is in the church-related college that these values are interpreted and cultivated. In them all the traditions and rich heritages of the Christian faith can be readily stressed. While it is not proper to say that the recognition of such values is limited to the Church's program of education, yet its institutions have in a unique way the responsibility for the fostering of the great spiritual ideals that Christian people have cherished. In a church-related college the study of religion may furnish the unity needed for a complete educational program.[4]

In listing the contributions that Presbyterian colleges have made, it would be unfortunate if we left the impression that we are belittling the Christian quality of the work being done in the state colleges and private non-church colleges and universities. Far from it. It is heartening to see a swelling tide of Christian leadership emerging from our state colleges. Faculty members and students alike, in great numbers, consecrate themselves to Christian ways of life in these colleges.

## How Is a Christian College Different?

The question is sometimes asked, even by members of the Presbyterian Church, "How is the Christian college different?" Certainly we must not lose sight of the fact that the basic purpose of the Christian college, like that of the tax-supported institution, is *education*. Dr. Samuel R. Spencer, Jr., Dean of Students at Davidson, wrote:

> Training the minds of young men and women is the primary function of the Christian college, as of any college. This by no means implies that the church college ignores such important areas as character, physical education, and social adjustment. On the contrary, it willingly accepts responsibility in these areas. The fact remains, however, that if the church college cannot offer training equivalent to that of the secular college on the same academic level, it has no justification for existence as an educational institution.[5]

We will not in our enthusiasm for the church college give the impression that these institutions have, in the past or present, succeeded in achieving those standards of excellence, either in education or in character training, which are idealized and expected by the Church and by the public at large. In all fairness we must not overlook the fact that too often piety has been substituted for academic excellence. Even now not a few church-related colleges are struggling with academic standards which are less than should be permitted in a school which bears the name of Christian. Not only so, but we have too often allowed the life of our campus to become more identified with the worldly standards about us than with the Christian community. Too often one sees or hears of practices on church college campuses which are only slightly different from, and in some cases little better than, those of other institutions or of the surrounding community.

I would say in complete frankness to our ministers and church officers and parents that the colleges can never reach their ideal in building Christian character, in creating a vital honor system, in preventing drinking and gambling, until the leaders of the Church and the parents of our students support us by their example. It is a tough assignment to sit in the chair when the executive committee of the faculty is dismissing a young man for a mild case of drinking on the campus, and to hear him say with all sincerity, "I have done nothing here that I do not do regularly with my parents in my home." This is not to excuse the college from its responsibility, but it is to plead for the consistency of the officers and members of the Church in their example and daily practice.

And yet, when all these qualifying statements are made about the Christian life of the church college, there *is* a difference; and perhaps a statement of these differences, real and potential, is in order. To begin with, members of the boards of trustees of our institutions are Christian men and women. They are representatives of the Church. They are aware of the ideals and purposes of these colleges. It is their responsibility, therefore, to formulate policies and provide administrators and leaders who can and will see that these ideals are realized.

Furthermore, the administrations and faculties of these colleges are chosen with due reference to their Christian faith and character. The church college is not only permitted but is even obligated to inquire closely into the faith and life of its teachers. Undoubtedly the most distinctive feature of the church-related college is its choice of faculty members. The men and women whose privilege and responsibility it is to teach young people day in and day out are the persons who set the tone of an institution. In the church school and state school both, the faculty member is considered for his knowledge of his field, for his proficiency in teaching, and for his character. An outstanding faculty member in a state university remarked, "But in a state institution, the likelihood is that these qualities are considered in the order listed. In the church college, while all three remain important, the order of emphasis is likely to be reversed."

Another difference is the usual basis of teaching. In the state college, teaching generally starts with knowledge of the subject matter. While the teacher himself may be an ardent Christian, he is likely to confine himself mostly to the area of information and knowledge, even though he may recognize that behind such a sub-

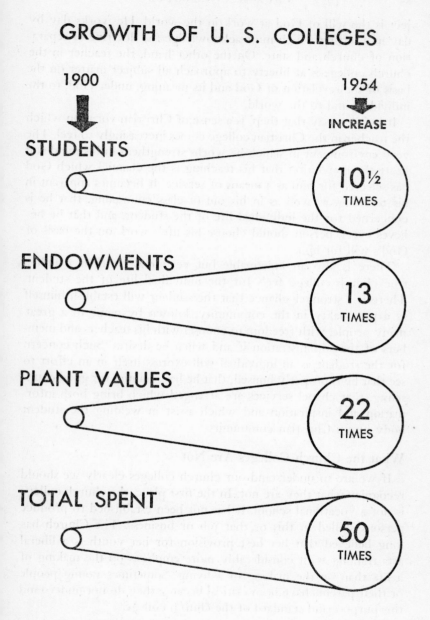

# GROWTH OF U. S. COLLEGES

1900             1954

INCREASE

**STUDENTS**

10½ TIMES

**ENDOWMENTS**

13 TIMES

**PLANT VALUES**

22 TIMES

**TOTAL SPENT**

50 TIMES

ject is the will of God at work in the world. He works day by day in a setting which must acknowledge the doctrine of separation of church and state. On the other hand, the teacher in the church college is at liberty to approach all subject matter on the basis of the revelation of God and its meaning, under God, to the individual and to the world.

It is fair to say that there is a sense of Christian vocation which the teacher in the Christian college comes increasingly to feel. The very environment in which he works strengthens in his mind and heart the conviction that his teaching is the channel which God has selected for him as a means of service. It becomes apparent in his teaching, as well as in his out-of-class counseling, that he is concerned for the individual life of the student, and that he believes every person should choose his life's work on the basis of God's will for him.

There is also an indefinable but very real concern which a true church college feels for the individual life of the student. There is a stronger chance that the student will establish himself as a personality in the community, known by name to a great many people, with freedom to counsel with his teachers and members of the administration if and when he desires. Such concern for the student as an individual will express itself in an effort to see that he is properly housed; that he has facilities for good counseling; that chapel services are arranged which bring both information and inspiration and which assist in welding the student body into a Christian community.

## What the Church Colleges Are Not

If we are to understand our church colleges clearly we should recognize what they are not. In the first place, the church college is not a vocational school. It has not been established to produce persons skilled in this or that job or business. The Church has long believed that her best provision for her youth is a liberal arts training with considerably more emphasis on the making of a life than on the making of a living. Sometimes young people or their parents have been critical because they do not understand this purpose and standard of the church college.

In the second place, the church college is not a substitute for the community junior college which is ordinarily open to all young men and women who have finished high school. The church college has as one of its distinctive opportunities and responsibilities the right to select its students. The community junior college has rendered a splendid service and will likely be much more in evidence in American education in the decades ahead when the rising tide in college enrollment is felt. It is expected, of course, that the church college can and will do something to help in meeting the enrollment problem; but it will defeat its purpose if it undertakes to absorb to the limit all students who knock at its doors for admission.

And in the third place, the church college is not a technical or a mechanical school. There are basic courses that are offered which have value in later training for technical life. Some of our colleges have working arrangements with technical schools, such as engineering, in which the college co-operates with the student in majoring in those areas which will best fit him for his later study in that field. In our institutions we have faculty committees for advising students who are headed toward medicine or law or theology, but by and large the college is not engaged in pre-professional training.

## The Significance of the Church College for the Future

The principal function of the church college is to provide a sound liberal arts training, furnishing the student with a basic understanding of the arts and sciences and humanities. Here he comes to a knowledge of the past through history and the languages. Here he discovers an appreciation of the cultural values which have their part in the development of personality and in the enabling of a man to relate himself to his fellow men. Here he studies philosophy and psychology and sociology. All these studies are supported by a knowledge of the Bible, which he would not be likely to obtain apart from such an institution. In short, the church college provides those values which are intended to help a student in making a satisfying and useful life, and in rendering a noble and unselfish service to humanity.

The church college which carries out this basic function has a powerful significance for the days to come. If these are the colleges which have set the pace of education in America in the past, so may they do it in the future. Woodrow Wilson once remarked that education had always produced its best results when associated with religion and that so far as he knew, education had not been associated in any major way with any religion other than Christianity. The problem which looms on our horizon is not primarily the making of a living, but rather the discovery of how we are to live together. The threat of war keeps us unsettled and fearful and will do so until it can be removed. This hallowed end will not be attained by armaments but rather by spiritual means. "Not by might, nor by power, but by my spirit, saith the Lord."[6] The Church and the public have a right to expect that from these church colleges will come persons with the insight, the spirit, and the unselfish devotion to lead in the direction of world understanding and world peace. Where shall we expect to find such leadership if not in the colleges which draw their students from the best of Christian homes and which can provide them with the best of Christian training? The commodity most needed in America today is moral character and spiritual integrity. This commodity is the natural fruitage of Christian education.

## The Church's Support of Her Colleges

No college can operate without assistance from some source. For the state institution support comes as taxes. Millions of dollars are assessed of us as citizens to make possible the universities. The church college charges in tuition and fees roughly one half the actual cost of education apart from buildings, grounds, and equipment. Individuals of means and with unselfish devotion to good causes have done much to make possible our church colleges. But it is not enough that a college barely balance its budget, or that funds come in from other and diverse sources through the patient and persistent efforts of college presidents. In the last analysis the Church must stand loyally behind its colleges and support them as its own.

We Presbyterians need a stronger sense of responsibility for

Christian higher education. Our members should know our colleges better. They should turn the attention of our finest boys and girls to these institutions. The colleges stand constantly in need of the earnest prayers of the Church. Do not expect them to make bricks without straw. Financial support for many of our institutions is the key to their success in the things they are attempting to do. The surest way for a Church to lose its colleges is to assume that the support can be had elsewhere. The danger may be that it can and will. There are many educational institutions in the nation today which were church-related a few years ago. The denominations to which they were related were irresponsible in support. Individuals and foundations which had little or no interest in the Church's ideals eventually came into the picture. Gradually, but surely, these colleges were lost to the Church. President Thurman Kitchin, formerly of Wake Forest College, once remarked in this connection: "I am frequently saying to the Baptists, you can have your colleges if you want them. If you do not want them, you will not have them."

Let us say with understanding, "I believe in Christian education." And let us act accordingly.

## CHAPTER 5

## ERNEST TRICE THOMPSON

Professor of Church History and Polity, Union Theological Seminary, Richmond, Va., 1925—.

B.A., Hampden-Sydney College, 1914, and D.D., 1926. M.A., Columbia University, 1915. B.D., Union Theological Seminary, 1920. Hoge Fellow, Union Theological Seminary, 1920-21. Litt.D., Washington and Lee University, 1933.

Moderator, Synod of Virginia, 1931 and 1940.

Associate Editor, *Presbyterian of the South*, 1931-37. Editor, *Presbyterian Outlook*, 1943-46; co-editor, 1946—.

Author of several books and frequent contributor to periodicals.

Chaplain in World War I.

# The Presbyterian Mark: An Educated Leadership

## YOUR SEMINARIES AND TRAINING SCHOOL

## E. T. Thompson

A PRESBYTERIAN congregation has lost its pastor.

What kind of minister does the pulpit committee hope to find as his successor?

Some committees demand unusual and unexpected qualifications: for example, the committee which recently specified that the minister must be "at least six feet tall and neither he nor any member of his family must ever attend the movies." Oddly enough, such a minister—one who had no children—was discovered.

Studies made a few years ago revealed that the average pulpit committee (not specifically Presbyterian) was concerned with a prospective minister's qualifications, first, as a leader (personality, spirituality, and adaptability being mentioned as most desirable, in that order); second, as a preacher; and third, as an administrator.

Today a pulpit committee might rank these qualifications in different order, and add still others to the list. The minister's work is manifold. He is required to preach, and his sermons must hold the interest and meet the needs of a wide variety of people. He is expected to teach as well as preach; and not only to teach, but also to supervise the total educational program of the church, involving the training of children, youth, and adults. He must in addition be skilled in the art of public worship, leading the worshipers, through his prayers and conduct of the service, into the presence of God. The minister's pastoral responsibilities have always been an important part of his calling, but never more so than today, when so many look to him for spiritual counsel. He must also be an administrator and a diplomat, if the machinery of

*Today's needs demand an educated ministry*

the church is to operate smoothly. Moreover, in many communities he is expected to exercise leadership in a wide variety of community affairs.

No minister can measure up fully to the ideal, and few fulfill all the expectations of their congregations. But Presbyterian ministers compare not unfavorably with those of other denominations. With rare exceptions, they have degrees from both college and theological seminary. Increasing numbers pursue additional graduate studies. It is not surprising that they have in their congregations a higher-than-average percentage of college-trained men and women, of professional men and women, of the intelligent and responsible leaders of the community.

Not all Presbyterians know that our Church's emphasis upon an educated ministry has a long tradition back of it, and that, from the beginning, it was a characteristic of their denomination.

## Beginnings of Ministerial Education

In the Middle Ages, priests needed only enough learning to stumble through the Mass. But the Reformation was based on a rediscovery of the Gospel, and Protestant ministers were expected to preach the Word of God as revealed in Scripture. The founding fathers of the Reformed and Presbyterian Churches felt that the sermons of a preacher who was ignorant of the Bible and of the leading doctrines of the Christian faith would have little value and might be positively harmful. A minister needed to know the original languages in which the Scriptures were written, and to be well grounded not only in theology, but also in related fields, such as ethics and philosophy. A candidate was not ordained as a Presbyterian minister until he was examined on these and other subjects by the Presbytery, composed of both ruling and teaching elders.

These high requirements for the ministry were brought from the old countries by the founders of the Presbyterian Church in America. The infant Church depended at first upon the universities of Scotland for their trained ministers, but soon it began to build its own educational institutions. First of these was William Tennent's so-called "Log College," founded in 1728, about twenty-five miles north of Philadelphia. Although this Log College was humble in structure and primarily a one-man institution, it educated a number of ministers who were responsible for the growth of the Presbyterian Church in the Middle Colonies.

The first real college of the Presbyterian Church was the College of New Jersey, now Princeton University, from which the Presbyterian Church drew most of its ministers in the Colonial period and for some time thereafter. Hampden-Sydney, the first Presbyterian institution of higher education in the South, opened its doors on January 1, 1776.

But a college education did not suffice for the making of a Presbyterian minister, even though some training in the Bible and in Christian beliefs was given to all college students. As early as 1761 the Presbyterian Synod—our highest court in that period —ruled that every student, after having obtained his first degree in college, should spend one year under the care of some minister who was skilled in theology, "to discuss difficult points in divinity, study the sacred Scriptures, form sermons, lectures, and such other useful exercises as he may be directed to in the course of his studies." Most doctors and lawyers in this period received whatever professional training they had by attaching themselves in similar fashion to some established doctor or lawyer. But this method proved unsatisfactory for all three professions. Only successful ministers were desired as teachers, and successful ministers were too busy to teach effectively. So presbyteries and synods began designating certain men to teach candidates, compensating them for their time.

Since clergymen of scholarly proclivities headed the educational institutions of the Church, it was natural that they should be employed in this capacity. The following action was taken in April, 1806:

> The Presbytery of Hanover taking into consideration the deplorable state of our country in regard to religious instruction, the very small number of ministers possessing the qualifications required by the Scriptures, and the prevalence of ignorance and error, on motion resolved:
>
> 1. That an attempt be made to establish at Hampden-Sydney College a complete theological library for the benefit of students in divinity.
>
> 2. That an attempt be also made to establish a fund for the education of poor and pious youth for the ministry of the gospel.

It was the opportunity to serve as head of this budding theological school that induced the Reverend Moses Hoge in the following year to go to Hampden-Sydney as president. In August, 1812, he wrote: "We have now nine or ten who intend to preach the Gospel, and about the same number of my alumni are now preaching."

Three years earlier the General Assembly had requested the presbyteries to vote whether they preferred one theological seminary for the entire Church, or one in the North and another in the South, or a seminary for each synod. The first choice prevailed, and Princeton Theological Seminary was founded in 1812. It remains the leading seminary of the Presbyterian Church, U.S.A., to the present time.

The Synod of Virginia was convinced, however, that a northern seminary would not supply the needs of the South for ministers, and in this same year, 1812, it "unanimously resolved on the establishment of a theological seminary [within its own borders] and unanimously concurred in the appointment of Dr. Hoge as their professor." Satisfactory arrangements were made with the trustees of the college by which Dr. Hoge could perform the duties of both the presidency of Hampden-Sydney and the synod's professorship of theology, and for the remaining eight years of his life he prosecuted the work with signal ability and success, sending more than thirty young men from his classes into the ministry.

Dr. Hoge died in 1820. Unable apparently to secure a successor, the Synod of Virginia seemed ready to abandon its experiment and throw its support to the General Assembly's institution at Princeton. Dr. John Holt Rice, pastor of the First Presbyterian Church in Richmond, strenuously opposed this move. He pointed out that students graduating in Princeton could not be persuaded to settle in the South, and moreover were not fitted to secure the best results in this region. On the other hand, he wrote, "the majority of students in the South will not go North. I think this is a settled point. In the State of North Carolina there are twelve to fifteen candidates for the ministry, now studying divinity in the old field school way. And between preachers brought forward in this manner and those who have better opportunities there is growing up a strong spirit of envy and jealousy on the part of the former."[1] A seminary in the South, Dr. Rice argued, was essential to the advancement of Presbyterianism in this region. Almost alone he persuaded the Presbytery of Hanover to continue its great experiment. In 1822 he himself was asked to develop the institution. His health was bad; he doubted whether he ought to accept such a heavy responsibility, but he could not escape it, and ended by accepting the call.

Dr. Rice began his seminary in a small house loaned by President Cushing of Hampden-Sydney, with three students. His immediate task was to secure more students, and then find the means to support them; to build dormitories and classrooms for the students and residences for the faculty; to build a library; to instruct his students in all branches of theological education; to raise funds from all quarters for the enlargement and permanent endowment of the institution; and last but not least, to win for the seminary the support of the Presbyterians of Virginia and North Carolina.

The task seemed impossible of fulfillment. But by almost superhuman labors Dr. Rice accomplished it in the seven years that remained of his life. He obtained a library, a building for lecture rooms, chapel and dormitories, two residences, three instructors, and nearly forty students. In addition there was a goodly endowment providing for the satisfactory maintenance of the school. Best of all, the seminary had back of it the unanimous support of the Synods of Virginia and North Carolina. It had become in fact, as well as in name, Union Theological Seminary. It was the only theological seminary south of Princeton between the Atlantic and the Pacific.

The Synods of South Carolina and Georgia in the beginning looked to Princeton rather than to the Virginia seminary for their supply of ministers, and raised a considerable sum for the endowment of a professorship in the former. But it soon became apparent to leaders in the deep South, as it had to Dr. Rice earlier in Virginia, that the South would have to train its own ministers. As the Missionary Society of the Synods of South Carolina and Georgia said in 1826:

We almost despair of being able to do anything efficiently in the Domestic Department of our Society unless missionaries can be raised up at home. We have too long looked to the North for a supply. The many vacancies that here occur, and the vast openings to the West, are more than sufficient to employ all the ministers that can be educated at the North for more than a hundred years to come; and there seems to be little in the South inviting to our Northern brethren. They dread our climate—our summers are considered as fatal to strangers. They also in general exceedingly dislike the domestic circumstances of our country, and few can reconcile it to their feelings to settle permanently in the South.[2]

To meet the growing demand of its own territory, Columbia Theological Seminary was established at Columbia, South Carolina, and its first professor, Dr. Thomas Goulding, was inaugurated on March 17, 1830. A favorite rule, which Dr. Goulding often impressed upon his students, was: "Let every sermon preached contain so much of the plan of salvation that should a heathen come in who had never heard the Gospel before, and who should depart, never to hear it again, he should learn enough to know what he must do to be saved."[3]

Union and Columbia Theological Seminaries between them could not begin to supply the number of ministers needed in the older sections of the South, much less in the rapidly growing West.

The great immigration into the Mississippi basin set in immediately after the close of the Revolutionary War. At the outset the Presbyterians held the strategic advantage. They were the second largest denomination in America, and in addition they had formed a Plan of Union with the Congregationalists—the largest denomination—in which these two Churches agreed to pool their resources for evangelizing the West. Because the Presbyterians had the superior organization, it turned out that practically all the churches founded in the middle tier of colonies by both Presbyterian and Congregational missionaries and composed of either Scotch-Irish or Puritan stock came into the Presbyterian Church. In addition, when the great migration began, the Scotch-Irish occupied the strategic areas on the frontier. As Theodore Roosevelt pointed out in his *Winning of the West*, they were "the first and the last set of immigrants to plunge into the wilderness." Because the Scotch-Irish led the rush into the West, the Presbyterian Church was among the first to send out missionaries to follow them with the Gospel.

But though Presbyterians drew ahead of Congregationalists, Episcopalians, and Quakers in occupying the West for Christ, they fell far behind both Baptists and Methodists. For example, Kentucky, the first state to be admitted from west of the mountains, and one which had been settled largely by Scotch-Irish with Presbyterian background, had in 1820 a total population of 563,317. The church population for this same year was only a little more than 46,000. Of this number, the Baptists and Methodists had about 21,000 each; while the Presbyterians had only 3,700, not one fifth the number of the other two.

Presbyterians fell behind Baptists and Methodists in the South because of a lack of ministers. In Scotland and in the North of Ireland religion and education had been inseparably combined. But in America, and especially in the South, the population was scattered, competent teachers were rare, the minds of the people were often diverted from their books by their circumstances in life, primary education was not universally provided, institutions of higher learning were not readily accessible, college-trained men, the sort demanded by Presbyterians, could not be found in any sufficient number, especially in the new West. Baptists and Methodists, who had no such educational qualifications, but demanded only a genuine religious experience and a desire to preach, found missionaries in abundance. It has been truly said that "illiteracy in the pulpit was repulsive to the educated few; but the masses welcomed men like themselves in whom knowledge of books was not expected, but whose sincerity and zeal was unquestionable."

The Presbyterian insistence on an educated ministry, however, had its compensations. The training of Presbyterian ministers, though it unfitted them somewhat for a popular appeal to the masses, enabled them to reach the intelligent and thoughtful minority in every community they entered. As a leading church historian has pointed out, the Presbyterian Church, in 1837, was the most influential . . . religious body in the United States. It represented in its ministry and membership the two most masterful races on the Continent, the Puritan colonists and the Scotch-Irish immigrants; and the tenacity with which it had adhered to the tradition, derived through both these lines, of admitting none but liberally educated men to its ministry, had given it exceptional social standing and control over men of intellectual strength and leadership.[4]

Presbyterian ministers also became the instructors of the people and did far more than any other denomination to establish educational institutions in both South and West.

In a period of rapid expansion, when trained ministers were not available, the refusal of the Presbyterian Church to lower the educational qualifications for its ministers was its weakness. But it was also—in that age, as throughout its history—the source of its strength.

## Founding of Additional Seminaries

As the Church grew and its resources permitted, additional seminaries were founded to serve other sections of the Church.

A need for a seminary in the country west of the Alleghenies had been felt and expressed for many years. Finally, in 1853, the General Assembly of the then undivided Church adopted a resolution looking to the establishment of a seminary in Danville, Kentucky, to serve the interests of synods both north and south of the Ohio River. The seminary opened that fall with three professors and twenty-three students. In its first eight years it seemed as though it might become one of the great training centers for Presbyterianism. The outbreak of the Civil War, however, doomed all such hopes. Danville Seminary passed into the hands of the Presbyterian Church, U.S.A., and Southern students attended other institutions.

The Synod of Kentucky (Southern) attempted for many years to persuade other synods to join it in establishing a seminary. In 1892, the Synods of Kentucky and Missouri agreed to establish such a seminary in Louisville. "The deepest interest has been shown in this work throughout Kentucky and Missouri, and in fact through the whole Southwestern Presbyterian Church," Dr. Hemphill reported to the newly appointed Board of Directors. "No one of the institutions for the training of young men for the ministry in this Church is situated in a large and growing city. Louisville . . . has many advantages . . . The students while securing their scholastic equipment will have abundant and varied forms of Christian work which will provide practical training of incalculable value."[5] The new institution opened on October 2, 1893, and three years later sent its first graduates into the ministry.

The advantages enjoyed by a theological seminary in a large city became apparent soon thereafter to the trustees of Union Theological Seminary at Hampden-Sydney. The main building of the seminary there was a long structure four stories high. The upper three stories were used for dormitories, each room being heated by an open fireplace. Students chopped their own wood, carried the fuel to their rooms, and built their fires. If a bath was desired, the student had to go down and pump water out of a cistern or well, carry it to his room, build a fire, heat up one bucket of water, use the other bucket for cooling purposes, take his bath in a wooden tub, and then dispose of the water—usually in the handiest way, that is, out the window. Opponents of change argued that if ministerial students ever got into steam-heated buildings and into porcelain tubs, they would be spoiled for home mission work. Others earnestly contended that ministerial students could never withstand the temptations of a large city.

In spite of such warnings, Union Seminary moved to Richmond, Virginia, in 1898, and entered upon a new period of expansion. A city not only offered better material facilities and greater financial support, but also more opportunities for practical work—preaching, teaching, counseling, and the like—which soon became an important part of the young minister's training.

For many years there was a growing sentiment among members of the two Presbyterian synods in Kentucky that their educational work should be combined, if their institutions were to be properly supported and if Presbyterianism was to regain the educational lead which it had formerly possessed. This goal was reached in 1901 when Central University (U. S.) in Richmond, Kentucky, was combined with Centre College (U.S.A.) in Danville; and Danville Seminary (U.S.A.) united with Louisville Seminary (U.S.) in Louisville.

It took much work on the part of the leaders to get the agreement to consolidate these institutions. There was opposition in the synod and also in the General Assembly. One protest, entered on the Minutes of the General Assembly, declared: "We deplore the consolidation because it is a serious menace to the peace of the Church. We apprehend trouble in bringing together in the board and in the faculty men of diverse views representing different churches . . . We now hold pleasant fraternal relations with the Northern Church, and we deplore any disturbance in the work allotted to us in the providence of God."[6]

Fortunately the authors of this protest proved to be poor prophets. When the Seminary celebrated the fiftieth anniversary of its consolidation, Dr. Benjamin J. Bush, the oldest Board member, testified that in all his years as a director, despite differences of judgment registered in votes of the Board, he had never known a vote to reflect denominational differences.

Columbia Theological Seminary, unable to care properly for its growing student body, moved in 1927 to Decatur, Georgia, where larger financial support was available, and where it could more efficiently serve its controlling synods. It is now strategically located in one of the most rapidly growing metropolitan areas of the South, and in the center of a territory stretching from the Mississippi River to the Atlantic Ocean and from the North Carolina line to Key West.

A fourth seminary, meanwhile, had been established in the growing Southwest. Texas was admitted to the Union in 1845. In 1850 this vast expanse of territory had a population of only 212,000; in 1870 the number had increased to 818,000; in 1900 to three millions, in 1930 to six millions, and in 1950 to seven and three-quarter millions.

As late as 1880 it was felt that it would be more profitable for Texas to send its candidates to the old seminaries in the North and East, paying a part of their expenses, than to undertake a theological school of its own. But it soon became apparent that the Southwest must have its own institution. As a committee reported to the Synod in 1894:

> We have forty candidates for the ministry and have had an average of about that number for several years past. These young men ... go east of the Mississippi River to take their theological course, and so far, few of them have returned. The indications now are that if we would retain our young men at home and supply our churches with a native ministry, we must at an early date found a Trans-Mississippi Seminary, in which our candidates will have all the advantages now enjoyed in the best seminaries of our land.[7]

From 1884 to 1895 a class in theology was conducted in Austin, Texas, by Dr. R. K. Smoot, pastor of the church in Austin, and Dr. R. L. Dabney, professor in the University of Texas. During this period some twenty-two men were trained and sent to serve in Texas. On October 1, 1902, Austin Theological Seminary, regarded as the outgrowth of this undertaking, opened its doors. Six out of the forty candidates under the care of Texas presbyteries were on hand for the opening class.

Thus, by the beginning of the present century the Presbyterian Church, U. S., had established the four theological institutions on which it now depends almost entirely for its supply of ministers.

Each of these seminaries is now owned and controlled by the group of synods which it normally serves: Austin, by the Synods of Texas, Oklahoma, Louisiana, and Arkansas; Columbia, by the Synods of South Carolina, Georgia, Florida, Alabama, and Mississippi; Louisville, by the Synods of Kentucky, Tennessee, Missouri, Appalachia, and Alabama in the U. S. Church, and Florida, Kentucky, and Mid-South in the U.S.A. Church; Union, by the Synods of Appalachia, North Carolina, Virginia, and West Virginia.

There were periods, especially during the depression years, when it seemed as if our denomination could not adequately support four theological seminaries; but recent developments have made it clear that our fathers built better than they knew.

At the turn of the century—1901—there were six candidates being trained for the ministry at Clarksville (the theological department of Southwestern University, later discontinued), twenty-three at Columbia, twenty-eight at Louisville, and seventy-two in Richmond—a total of one hundred twenty-nine. Twenty-five ministers were set aside to teach in these four institutions, an average of five students to each professor. In September, 1954, there were 107 undergraduates in Austin Seminary, 173 in Columbia, 123 in Louisville, and 199 in Union in Richmond—607 in all. There were forty-one professors, with an average of fifteen students to each.

The number of students rose sharply after World War I, decreased during the Great Depression, and rose slowly as the Church itself increased in membership. The great increase set in after World War II. In five years—1947-1952—the number of students at Columbia almost tripled; at Austin the number more than tripled; while at Louisville and Union there were more than twice as many students as there had been five years earlier. As the historian of Louisville Seminary explains:

> Ministerial students whose education had been interrupted by military service completed their college degrees and came on to Seminary in increasing numbers. As the acute shortage of ministers came to be felt in the Church at large during the war, youth leaders made renewed efforts to present to young men the call to the ministry. A general mood of moral and spiritual concern for the plight of mankind in a world made tense by "the cold war" produced ministerial candidates from among mature men already established in other vocations. As a result of these trends seminaries generally began to have unprecedented enrollments.[8]

One of the men who came during this period was Gary. He was born in Wales, went to sea, entered the Royal Navy, and rose to rank of Commander. He was torpedoed several times and had a conviction that he had been providentially spared. He gave up a promising executive career in a steamship line, came to this country, was graduated from college *summa cum laude*, served as student pastor to several mountain churches, and then entered the seminary.

Ralph was a New Englander. He became a captain in the Army Air Force, then entered the insurance business, which he gave up to prepare for the ministry. He felt a call to work with laboring people and is now serving a church in an industrial area, among a group not often represented in our Presbyterian churches in the South.

Bill was born on a farm, attended rural schools, and worked on farms and in the tobacco business. War took him to England, where a devout British layman turned Bill's mind toward religious matters. He began to take an active part in the religious activities at his military post. After his discharge, he entered college, was graduated *cum laude,* and went to the seminary.

Will is following a family tradition. Both grandfathers were Presbyterian ministers; his brother and brother-in-law are pastors of churches. He was graduated from college with Phi Beta Kappa rank, entered the seminary, and has been joined by his younger brother.

Ed comes from a coal miner's family. The town had no high school, but he earned money in the mines to go to school elsewhere and to graduate from college. In his first summer vacation after entering the seminary he took a truck and tent and went to a raw, new mine village with no church of any kind. He started a vacation Bible school for the children. At the end of the summer a group of fifty people petitioned the presbytery to organize a church.

Administrators thought for a while that the rapid increase in the number of ministerial candidates might be a temporary phenomenon, a flash set off by war. But a study of the situation reveals that the increase is almost certainly a permanent one, and that even more students may be expected in the future. For one thing, the Southern Presbyterian Church has greatly increased its membership and is growing rapidly. In 1901, when 129 ministerial candidates were studying in four theological institutions, the total membership of the Church was 229,642. In 1953, when 601 candidates were studying in four institutions, the total membership of the Church was 756,884. The increase in the number of ministerial candidates has done little more than keep pace with the growth of the Church. The number of young men in high school and college who have put themselves under the care of their presbyteries indicates that the enrollment at the four theological seminaries will continue to mount.

The increase in the student body has compelled our four theological seminaries to expand their facilities. As Union Theological Seminary reported to its constituency in 1952:

> The central fact about Union Theological Seminary's present situation is that it is a 100-man school doing a 200-man job. Moreover, there is every indication that it will be called upon to expand to the 250-man level in the near future.
>
> Right now—today—the Seminary is overloaded. For a time the crowding, the improvised measures, the too-large classes, and the other consequences [single rooms occupied by two men, for example; and double rooms by three] can be cheerfully accepted. For the future, however, a choice has to be made: Union must move either backward or forward. To go back to its former size means to refuse admission to many well-qualified candidates from our own presbyteries and to reduce the number of graduates sent into the field each year. The alternative is to expand the Seminary's plant and teaching staff in line with the larger task which confronts it.[9]

With the other seminaries of the Church also crowded to the doors, there was only one way out of the dilemma. The four supporting synods raised two and one-half million dollars, which enabled the Seminary to meet its most pressing needs. Austin, Columbia, and Louisville have likewise greatly increased their endowments. Three of the seminaries have built new dormitories and added air-conditioned libraries and other necessary facilities. The fourth, Louisville Seminary, finds its present plant altogether inadequate. A new campus site, one of the most choice spots in Louisville, has been purchased; and the Seminary is now engaged in a campaign for two million dollars to erect its new plant.

## Changes in Ministerial Training

The training of a minister has undergone some changes in the last fifty years. Life has become more complicated, and more is expected of a minister today than was the case half a century ago.

For a hundred years the required curriculum in our theological seminaries embraced four divisons: Bible, Church History, Systematic Theology, and Practical Theology. The last received little attention. When the writer began his seminary training in 1915 there was a course in Homiletics—the art of preaching—and one brief course on the Sunday School, and that was practically all. An instructor came in one month during the year and gave lessons in elocution. The course on pastoral theology was taken up with a study of the Pastoral Epistles, which did not give the student much help in facing the many pastoral duties which he would soon be required to assume.

Emphasis today is placed upon the Bible, as it was in the beginning. But this department and others have been enriched. Five men are teaching in the Bible department of one institution, where formerly there were two. A professor of Missions has been added in the historical department, and a professor of Christian Ethics to the department of Systematic Theology. The greatest expansion has occurred in the practical department. There are now three men here, with a fourth soon to be added, where a generation ago men in other departments gave only incidental courses as a sideline to those in which they were expert.

Men are now trained much more thoroughly in religious education, in pastoral theology, in the psychology of religion, in pastoral counseling, in the conduct of worship, in the preparation and delivery of sermons. Men able to give expert instruction are on hand through the year to help individual students make the best of their voices. Recording machines are used to enable the neophyte preacher to hear and evaluate his own delivery; soon he will be able to see himself conducting a service on the screen.

Students in the seminary have always engaged in field work of some sort—preaching, teaching, counseling, working with various age groups in one way or another. In recent years men have been added to theological faculties whose prime responsibility is to oversee these practical labors of the student, and to make them an essential part of his training, corresponding to the laboratory experience of a scientist or the clinical training of a physician. A student during the academic year is assigned such part-time work, and in the summer whole-time work, as in the judgment of his director will mean the most for his future usefulness as a minister. And he is not left to work out his problems alone.

An important step forward was taken when full-time librarians were added to the seminary staff. Under their prodding, gentle or otherwise, library facilities have been improved, modern buildings erected with good lighting, comfortable chairs, reading rooms for general use, and carrels for specialized labors. The stock of books increases constantly. In 1901 one seminary had 18,000 volumes; in 1954 there were more than 70,000 volumes on its shelves, with approximately three thousand new titles being added annually. In all our theological libraries, the best of the older volumes are available to students, and all the important new ones, as well as significant religious publications. Students are sent to the library and encouraged to read, in a way that was not possible before men trained in library science were on the seminary staff.

After three years in one of our theological seminaries, the young minister is able to study the Scriptures in the original languages and is conversant with the several English translations; he has spent entire quarters on the minute study of key sections and books, and has been introduced to the Biblical teachings as a whole. He has studied the history, organization, government, and missionary activity of the Church from the days of the Apostles down to our own time. He has been led into a comprehension of the Christian faith as an orderly and harmonious structure of belief, and is prepared to defend its essential truthfulness. He has been trained, with the best of modern aids, in the theory and practice of religious education, evangelism, worship, preaching, and pastoral work. He has spent half of the week ends of his school year and two of his summers in "laboratory work"—actual practice in the field, supplying pulpits in rural and urban churches, teaching Sunday school classes, leading young people's groups, making evangelistic team trips, calling at hospital bedsides, visiting prisons, or assisting in social welfare activities.

For several years our theological seminaries, together with those of other denominations, have recognized an obligation to aid ministers, in whatever religious work they are engaged, to continue their theological education. Each of our seminaries awards a number of fellowships (though none of them has a sufficient number) which enable their best students to continue their education at home or abroad. Each seminary now makes some provision for graduate work, whereby a minister can earn his Master's degree after one or more years of study, or his Doctor's degree after three or more years. Most of these graduate students carry on their work with no break in their pastorates, fulfilling their residence requirements in the summer, or in broken intervals during the regular seminary session.

### Providing Lay Workers: The Training School

Fifty years ago need began to be felt for trained lay workers—especially women—in the full-time service of the Church. The idea of having a training school for such workers originated in the mind of Dr. A. L. Phillips, Superintendent of Sunday Schools and Young People's Work from 1903 to 1915. Traveling throughout the Assembly, he saw the need for more and better trained workers. In response to his plea, and to an overture from the Presbyterian Committee of Publication, the General Assembly in 1911 appointed a committee to study the question of founding a training school to be owned and controlled by the General Assembly.

Three years later the General Assembly's Training School began operations with fewer than ten boarding students. Classes were held in the building of the Committee of Publication in Richmond. The student body increased rapidly, the material possessions and endowment of the school much more slowly. Today, the institution has an endowment of more than a million dollars and total assets of more than two million dollars. It has a well-furnished dormitory; a second building which contains dining room, chapel, social and recreational facilities; and has recently completed a superb new administration building. The school has been accredited by the Southern Association of Colleges and Secondary Schools, and by the American Association of Schools for Religious Education. The institution offers a two-year course, leading to a Bachelor's degree in religious education for students with two years of college work; and to the degree of Master of Religious Education for college graduates.

Graduates of the General Assembly's Training School serve as church secretaries, as directors of Christian education, as leaders of young people, as directors of music, as missionaries at home and abroad, as workers with college students, as Sunday school extension workers, as teachers of Bible in weekday religious education and in our church colleges; they have their place in every Board of the Church. In the more than forty years of its operation, over 2,500 alumni have gone from the Training School into the service of the Church; they live and serve today in every synod and in every foreign field in which our Church is at work.

The majority of Training School graduates have been women, but in recent years a growing number of men, planning to serve the Church as laymen rather than as ministers, have been enrolled.

A careful study made in 1943 revealed that the average length of service of women entering full-time church work after graduation from the Training School was 5.7 years, after which they married and became volunteer workers in their own churches. Because of this fact, and because the demand for lay workers is constantly increasing, the number of Training School graduates is never sufficient for the demand.

## High Standards Have Proved Effective

In the early days on the frontier, when settlers were pouring into the Mississippi basin, the Presbyterian Church suffered numerical loss because of its insistence on an educated ministry. But even then, as we have seen, there were compensations.

Today the advantage—indeed, the necessity—of a trained leadership is more apparent. The educational status of the average American has been lifted. Men today, in the Church and out of the Church, are asking questions that demand intelligent answers: about the meaning of life, the destiny of the human race and its civilization, and the deeds of God in history and nature.

A careful study of theological education made a generation ago revealed that men with college and seminary training were from 40 to 75 per cent more effective in their ministry than those lacking such training. About the same time our seminaries discovered that men lacking proper qualifications were not acceptable to the Presbyterian constituency.

Thus Columbia Theological Seminary reported to the 1930 General Assembly:

> We feel that the Presbyteries . . . should be urged to exercise great care and to accept as candidates for the ministry only men who are of sound health, good character, and thorough preparation . . . It is becoming more and more difficult for men who are inadequately prepared to meet the requirements of our curriculum. . . . It is also becoming more difficult to place such men in the churches after they have completed their work in the Seminary.[10]

President Cunningham about the same time reported that a new policy of Louisville Seminary called for "our denying admission to a considerable number of students during the past year, and the dropping of some men who were enrolled. We believe it a far larger service to the Church to prepare, if necessary, fewer men who are thoroughly equipped than to continue to allow young men of lesser endowments and inadequate scholastic preparation to graduate."

Today, it is very rare for any of our theological institutions to accept any student who lacks his academic degree. Moreover, there is a more careful system of recruiting ministerial candidates. Each seminary student is carefully appraised, not only on the basis of his academic work, but also regarding his personality and field work. Deficiencies revealed are handled where possible through counseling. If it appears that the student is not qualified to render effective service in the ministry, he is dropped.

The General Assembly's Training School also is gradually raising its standards, and an increasing proportion of its students are college graduates.

These carefully trained ministers and lay workers are proving their worth now, and will do so even more in the days that lie ahead. For the South has entered upon a period of rapid development that has been called the "most dramatic regional transformation since the opening of the West or the War between the States."[11] Agriculture is being diversified and mechanized. Industry is growing, and this calls for a parallel expansion in transportation, building, retailing, and professional services. Per capita income in the South is increasing faster than in any other section.

People are moving from other regions into the South; and, within the South, from rural to urban areas and from the center of the city into the suburbs and outskirts. Cities and metropolitan areas are growing much more rapidly in the South than in the nation as a whole. All available evidence indicates that this growth will continue.

The changing South offers the Church an unparalleled opportunity, particularly in the rapidly growing suburban areas. "The most important population movement in America," writes one of our urban sociologists, "is from the cities into the adjoining areas. The people who are making their homes in these nascent communities generally have a Protestant heritage (this is especially true in the South). The wisdom displayed by ministers and laymen in adapting old churches or establishing new ones to serve the religious needs of this population will greatly influence the course of Protestantism for the next fifty years." This is an understatement; it will *determine* the course of Protestantism for generations to come. People in these growing suburbs want what the Presbyterian Church has to offer, and today as never before it attracts men from every religious background and with no religious background.

The Presbyterian Church lacks ministers. In 1954 it had 594 vacant churches; that is, one church in six had neither a regular minister nor a stated supply. In addition, there are great numbers of unfilled openings for assistant pastors, university pastors, chaplains, and missionaries for home and foreign fields. The openings for trained lay workers cannot even be estimated.

The fact that the supply is inadequate for the need, plus the fact that young men and women will respond to a challenge when it is clearly presented, and are even now doing so in increasing numbers, means that enrollment at the seminaries and Training School will continue to grow, that faculties will have to be enlarged (even now classes are too large for the best instruction), that facilities will have to be added, and that support will have to be expanded.

For many years theological seminaries made no charge for tuition and little for rent and board. During the depression of the

1930's they began, very reluctantly, to charge the students a small additional fee. Since then tuition costs have increased, but the students (as in any educational institution) pay only a modicum of the actual cost of their education.

The synods which own and control the various seminaries contribute annually a small percentage of their benevolence budget to their support. In the case of Union Theological Seminary, this amounts to about fourteen per cent of its yearly operating expenses. In the case of the other seminaries, it is little more. The Training School receives a portion of its budget from the benevolences of the General Assembly. The major part of the support of all these institutions comes from endowments, from occasional bequests, and from numerous gifts, both large and small.

Recent campaigns have demonstrated that many Presbyterians are not acquainted with the part that the seminaries and Training School play in the life of the Church. The campaigns have also made it clear that when Presbyterians are given the information and the opportunity, they will rise to their support and find joy in so doing.

## CHAPTER 6

*MALCOLM CHESTER McIVER*

Director, Department of Campus Christian Life, Division of Higher Education, Board of Christian Education, Richmond, Va., 1954—.

A.B., Centre College, 1941. B.D., Louisville Presbyterian Theological Seminary, 1944.

Minister to Students, University of Alabama, 1944-52.

Chaplain, active duty U.S.N.R., 1944-46.

Student, University of Edinburgh, Scotland, 1952-54; Ph.D. candidate.

# Campus Christian Life

## STUDENT RELIGIOUS WORK ON ALL CAMPUSES

## *Malcolm C. McIver*

GEORGE, a freshman enrolled in a large southern university, had difficulty in adjusting to his new campus environment.

"When I entered the university," he said, "my only ambition was to be outstanding in scholarship and in social life on the campus. I had been a leader in high school and I expected to continue this role in college. The props were soon knocked out from under me. I realized that I was in a strange new place which called for decisions on every hand. I was lonely and bewildered. I started thinking as I had never thought before. How should I spend my life? What is really important? Does God care about me now? These and similar questions suddenly became very real to me. I needed to talk with someone, but it seemed that no one would understand."

In the South, more than 50,000 Presbyterian students and 5,000 or more Presbyterian professors are on the campuses of colleges and universities; they constitute one of the great mission fields of the Church. Service to these students and professors is the particular concern of the Board of Christian Education, which has its offices in Richmond, Virginia. In 1950, the name of the Department of Student Work was changed to the Department of Campus Christian Life to signify that the Church is concerned not only with the students on a campus but also with the faculty and staff. Campus Christian Life is the Church at work on the college and university campuses of the South, in tax-supported institutions as well as in church-related and other private schools. Its program includes proclaiming the Gospel, and its goal is to win unbelievers for Christ while holding the interest and motivating the activities of Christian students.

In this work, the key organization is Westminster Fellowship and the key individual is the minister to students. Support of Campus Christian Life is officially centered in the synod, yet much help is given also by the churches in which the activities are centered.

George could be your son. There are many like him on every campus—lonely, confused, insecure—and the number increases each year. The student population in the United States has quadrupled since 1920 and more than doubled since 1938. It is estimated that from 1953 to 1970 there will be an increase in enrollment in our Southern colleges and universities ranging from 24 per cent in Arkansas to 150 per cent in Florida.

Today there is an evangelistic opportunity on the campus unparalleled at any time in the history of our Church. The Presbyterian Church has a responsibility not only to freshmen like George, but also to upper classmen, to graduate students, to young men and women from overseas, to members of faculties, and to the administrative staffs of the colleges. Here the primary task of the Church is to confront the entire academic community with the Good News of Jesus Christ.

William Temple said that to evangelize "is so to present Christ Jesus in the power of the Holy Spirit, that men shall come to put their trust in God through Him, to accept Him as their Saviour, and serve Him as their King in the fellowship of His Church."[1] Basically, evangelism on the campus is telling the Good News through worship, Bible study, fellowship, and service in such a way as to lead faculty and students to recognize the sovereignty of God in all of life, and to commit themselves to Christ in love and trust. This is not pious talk—it is the urgent concern of Campus Christian Life and of the Presbyterian Church.

In almost every college there are those who have never heard the Gospel presented in terms which speak to their understanding.

Some students and faculty members have heard the message and have rejected it. Still others believe, but do not feel the dynamic force of the Christian faith in their everyday campus life. The following example illustrates the opportunity before us.

In one of our Southern universities, each student files a religious preference card on registration day. The breakdown of these cards for 1954 included these preferences: Baptist, 2,463; Methodist, 2,410; Presbyterian, 831; Episcopal, 603; Jewish, 532; Roman Catholic, 501; Christian, 106; and Lutheran, 72. Many of the students who listed a church preference were not church members. More than 600 students indicated no church preference at all, and one student wrote across the face of his card, "Bunk." Surely, no one would deny that the campus is a strategic opportunity for the Church today.

## The Campus Situation: A Study in Contrasts

Our colleges and universities come in different sizes and shapes. At one extreme we have our four-year liberal arts church colleges; and at the other, the "street-car" college in a large metropolitan area. Within the bounds of our General Assembly, there are large state-supported universities enrolling thousands of

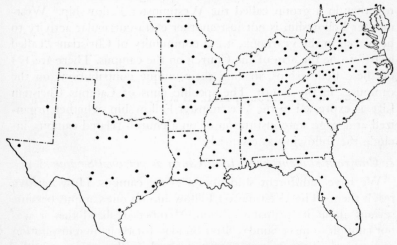

*Locations of Westminster Fellowships*

students; small (under 1,000 students) teachers colleges; and the ever-expanding schools of technology. The graduate institution and the junior college must be added to complete the picture.

The university today is no longer a community. It is broken into separate sub-communities—fraternity-sorority groups with special housing units, athletic groups high in campus prestige, various schools of specialization, agencies of student government, special interest groups including a multitude of clubs; and finally the professors, many of whom are set apart from the student and his personal needs. Not only do we find separate sub-communities, but "for many years the work of universities has tended to be done in an increasing number of separate water-tight compartments."[2] The lack of integration and the confusion concerning its basic function have caused the modern university to become a multiversity moving in many directions at once.

## Westminster Fellowship: An Arm of the Church

In the broken collegiate community, our students need the direction, the guidance, the encouragement, the inspiration, and the hope of the Christian faith. Campus Christian Life ministers through a church-centered community, and the students are drawn together in a group called the Westminster Fellowship.[3] Westminster Fellowship is not just another extra-curricular activity to be placed in the yearbook; it is a community of Christians "called apart" to be the arm of the Church on the campus. There are 173 of these Fellowships, making their unique contributions on the campuses in the South. The specific aims of Campus Christian Life as expressed in the Westminster Fellowship, whether organized at a large state institution or on a church-related campus, include the following as essentials:

*1. Confront students with Jesus Christ as personal Saviour.*

We have indifferent students on every campus. How can we reach them? The Westminster Fellowship on one campus became serious about its primary mission. Members realized that it was not enough to meet Sunday after Sunday for their own inspiration and growth; it was necessary to move back on the campus in order to reach the indifferent non-Christian students. The campus situation was studied carefully and strategic points of approach were selected:

(a) *Strategic individuals*—the president of the student body, a graduate student, the captain of the basketball team, an outstanding Moslem student from Turkey.

(b) *Strategic groups*—the cabinet of the student government, scholastic fraternities, the council for overseas students.

(c) *Strategic centers*—the housing units (dormitories, sororities, and fraternities), the student newspaper office, the soda shop.

(d) *Strategic infiltration*—the organization of quiet but efficient teams to call on students, especially those who stated no church preference.

*2. Train students to live and work within the life of the church.*

A principle of Campus Christian Life is that all campus work should be church-related. The Westminster Fellowship is not a church, but is related to a church alongside the campus, or to a group of churches nearby. Students are encouraged to participate in the program of the local church, and in most communities the Sunday morning service of worship is the heart of the Westminster Fellowship. An important part of our ministry to the campus is training students for church leadership and helping them to understand what God is doing in and through His Church in our day.

*3. Challenge students with a Christian interpretation of life by helping them to use Christian insight in their vocational plans.*

This includes not only planning for the jobs which they will later fill; it includes also the understanding that being a student is in itself a vocation. The major task of the Christian student is to be a student. He is not living a detached life in an ivory tower. He realizes that God has a definite purpose for his life on a particular campus. A Christian student who understands that God has called him to work with his mind does not select a course because it is easy. Thinking may be a form of worship; and study should take priority over all other campus activity for the Christian.

The Westminster Fellowship seeks to help students understand that every man is called to serve God in his work. The policeman, the farmer, the laborer, the minister, the doctor—God calls each man to do his job. In making his vocational plans, a Christian student considers these questions: "How can I best glorify God with my life?" "Shall I use my talents on the mission field?" "What are the needs for leadership in the Church?"

*4. Challenge students with a Christian interpretation of life by providing them with help as they consider establishing Christian homes.*

During the college year fundamental attitudes toward marriage are considered. What is Christian marriage? What are the proper motives for entering into marriage? What is the Christian interpretation of sex? How is a Christian family established?

This writer received a letter from a couple who learned the meaning of Christian marriage in the Westminster Fellowship. Here are some excerpts:

"This day, our third anniversary, finds us in———, attending as adult advisers the Youth Fellowship Rally. We are working almost full time in church activity with a few spare hours daily for law practice and other items. . . . We just wanted to drop in on you folks for a few minutes tonight and let you share with us the happiness we share together with our little girl, since you and the Westminster Fellowship had such a vital part in helping us onward toward all these wonderful experiences together."

*5. Guide students into active participation in the world-wide student Christian movement.*

The Presbyterian Church, U.S., has always believed in the holy catholic Church. The Westminster Fellowship, following the tradition of our Church, is a charter member of the United Student Christian Council which was founded in 1944. This council is the national federation of the YMCA, the YWCA, and eleven denominational student groups in the United States, enabling them to accomplish together things they could never do alone.

Through the United Student Christian Council, the Westminster Fellowship is a member of the World's Student Christian Federation—the international student Christian movement representing more than fifty countries. The Federation was founded in 1895 at Vadstena Castle, Sweden, by John R. Mott and representatives from four other countries. It was the first of the world ecumenical agencies, and in a real sense is the father of the World Council of Churches. Many present leaders of the World Council of Churches were active in the World's Student Christian Federation during their student days.

The Westminster Fellowship participates in the Federation by sending delegates to its committee meetings, by taking an active part in the World Day of Prayer for Students on the third Sunday in February, and by supporting the work of the Federation financially.

*6. Influence higher education for Christ and His Church.*

As the Church has continued to proclaim the Lordship of Christ over every aspect of individual and corporate life, so the ministry of Campus Christian Life seeks to present Christ's claims to higher education through its work with faculty members and administrative staffs.

One of the most thrilling developments in the Church today is the growth of Christian faculty groups.* Faculty members are key persons in producing an effective work on the campus. The students remain in college only four years, but professors spend a lifetime influencing and teaching generations of students. The same can be said of administrative officers. We must turn to the Christians in these groups for assistance. Through the Faculty Christian Fellowship, Presbyterian professors are encouraged to rethink their field of study and their professional relationships in terms of their faith.

It is the responsibility of the Westminster Fellowship to help bridge perhaps the sharpest gap in Christian community on the campus—the great chasm between students and faculty. "To make the community live, we must discover a means of bringing an

---

* A fuller account of this movement is given in Chapter 7.

intercommunion among Christian teachers and Christian students."[4] On many campuses this intercommunion is brought about by inviting faculty to speak to the Westminster Fellowship, by asking faculty to entertain students in their homes, and by organizing faculty-student groups to study particular problems of campus life and the Christian's responsibility in facing these problems. If we are to influence higher education for Christ and the Church, it will be necessary for students and faculty to join in the task of witnessing to the Lordship of Christ.

## Communicating the Gospel: Some Techniques

The ministry of Campus Christian Life through the Westminster Fellowship has high aims and purposes, but unless it succeeds in communicating the Gospel message to the campus it has failed in its task.

An excerpt from a letter written by a brilliant physics student will help us understand the importance of communication. He wrote:

> The era of following our own boys and girls to college merely to sustain them in the Church is past. We are here a part of a great missionary enterprise, and the campus is our mission field. The problems of communication are as difficult as if our students spoke Ubangi. We must use all kinds of means to win them into the Christian community—food, shelter, fellowship, worship, ping-pong, study, acceptance, intellectual probing—but finally we must face the responsibility of teaching an understandable, believable Christianity to these people. I don't mean that it must be watered down: heaven forbid. I mean we must speak it in their language. I mean we must face their questions, take their problems seriously, study their complaints and ailments.[5]

Ten years ago activities in Westminster Fellowship emphasized recreation and unusual programs in order to attract large numbers. Today the trend has shifted to intensified Bible study, seminars, study retreats, and the recruitment and training of students for Christian service and leadership in every area of life.

The study group technique is being used effectively to make the Gospel relevant on the campus. One Westminster Fellowship reports: "Several small study groups are emerging . . . one on personal evangelism, another studying the nature of the university . . . a fraternity group is discussing the Christian and alcohol."

On another campus the student government was changed as the result of a study group. "One student who disapproved of the political party system in the university found another of like mind and planned a reform. A new political party was formed with Christian principles, cutting across all lines in the university and based on real issues. The whole 'student party' slate went into office in the next election."

Another student saw the missionary opportunity with overseas students almost untapped, and started a system for becoming friends with them.

## The Minister to Students: Guide and Counselor

An important key to the success of a vital campus ministry lies in the personnel. "The work of campus Christian life is a special ministry requiring personnel who feel in a real sense a call to the missionary frontiers of the academic community."[6] There are thirty full-time and twenty-six part-time ministers to students and lay Campus Christian Life workers. In addition, there are 104 non-paid workers, including pastors, Directors of Christian Education, and advisers who give some time to guiding the program of Westminster Fellowship. These workers are able, alert, and well-trained. They stand ready to counsel personally or to aid both faculty and students.

The duties and responsibilities of the minister to students are legion:

He is a committed follower of Jesus Christ and a responsible member of the Church, professionally trained for a full-time ministry to the students and faculty of a modern university. He must have as much strength and skill in group work as in preaching, preferably more. He is evangelist, teacher, counselor, pastor, and friend. He will be acutely aware of the tensions and injustices that are driving the people to despair. He will be able to think as a Christian in the academic community and must be able to address the Gospel to that community of students, faculty, and administrators. He will be willing to trust individual students and faculty with Jesus Christ, which is another way of saying he will minister with patience, keep his mind open and receptive, and explore new ways in which the Christian Gospel is made relevant to individual and group life.[7]

---

## A Typical Week of a Minister to Students

His parish includes 946 Presbyterian students and 52 Presbyterian faculty members.

| | | |
|---|---|---|
| Sunday: | 9:45 a.m. | Teaches student Bible class. |
| | 11:00 a.m. | Sunday morning worship—preaching by the pastor or minister to students (25% of time), with both in the pulpit each Sunday. |
| | 6:00 p.m. | Student-led program and worship. |
| Monday: | 5:00 p.m. | Worship Commission planning session. |
| | 9:30 p.m. | Study group on "Prayer." |
| Tuesday: | 7:00 p.m. | Social Action Commission or Program Commission. |
| | 9:30 p.m. | Seminar on "Contemporary Theology." |
| Wednesday: | 6:00 p.m. | Study group on "World Religions." |
| | 7:00 p.m. | Outreach Commission planning session. |
| Thursday: | 7:00 p.m. | Westminster Fellowship Council meeting. |
| | 9:00 p.m. | Seminar on "The Reformed Tradition." |
| Friday: | 7:00 p.m. | Fellowship Commission occasionally meets at supper for planning. Periodic meetings of the Intercollegiate Christian Fellowship which brings together students from a number of campuses in the state. |
| Saturday: | | Occasional afternoon workcamps. |

The minister to students is in his office each morning of the week studying and thinking through his total ministry to the academic community. Much of his work day is used in counseling and visiting students and faculty on the campus. Able, alert, and well-trained, he is available to the campus community at all times.

---

During a recent visit to a large campus in Texas, the writer found a minister to students acting as unofficial chaplain to graduate students from overseas. This minister not only knew the names and family background of the overseas students, but he also was drawing many of them into the life and fellowship of the Church.

Another minister to students allocates about one fourth of his time to work with faculty. He is leading a group composed of young professors and graduate students in a study of contemporary theology.

The Presbyterian minister to students works closely with other full-time professional leaders on the campus. In some cases, the Presbyterian minister has taken the initiative in establishing a relationship with other ministers on the campus in order to work together "for the Christian good of the whole university community."[8]

On the majority of state campuses, the minister to students has excellent support and interest from the administration. While there are some non-Christians with teaching and administrative responsibilities, it is heartening to know that the faculty and administration in most state-controlled institutions are showing real concern about the religious life of their colleges. The president of a large college recently said: "I am convinced that the staff and faculty of this college cannot meet the deepest needs of our students. Only through a vital relationship with the Church and its work on the campus can these needs be satisfied."

The Dean of Students at one of the Southern universities is a voting member of the University Ministers' Council. This Council meets each month and basic problems concerning the campus community are discussed. During a recent spring term, the Ministers' Council sponsored a series of faculty luncheons at which Dr. Arnold Nash's book, *The University and the Modern World*, was studied.

The minister to students and the Campus Christian Life worker carry on their work not apart from, but within, the Presbyterian Church. Their services are provided by the Church "to the end that students and faculty may be brought into the fellowship of believers and learn to take their places in the life of the Church."[9]

## The Department of Campus Christian Life

Throughout the development of higher education many have called the campuses the world's most fertile mission field; nevertheless, only in recent years has the Church awakened to the tremendous opportunities in Campus Christian Life. The YMCA demonstrated to the Church the need for organized Christian work on the campuses. "Yet it was not until 1909 that Presbyterian student groups were begun on the campuses of two of our state-supported universities—Virginia Polytechnic Institute and the University of Texas." [10]

Dr. Henry H. Sweets has been called the "Father of Christian Higher Education in the Presbyterian Church, U. S." During his years of service as the Secretary of the Executive Committee of Christian Education and Ministerial Relief, he raised his voice prophetically for a Presbyterian ministry to the campus. In 1916 he "invited pastors in college communities to come together at the expense of his Committee to talk over their common problems." [11]

Twenty years later, student work (now Campus Christian Life) became one section of the Presbyterian Educational Association, composed of college church pastors, ministers to students, directors of student work, as well as others who had related responsibilities in the local college communities throughout the General Assembly. Meeting each summer since 1936, the Campus Christian Life Section of the Presbyterian Educational Association has come to be a time of fellowship, of practical learning, of deepening faith, and of broadening vision.

The ministry of Campus Christian Life did not receive official recognition by the General Assembly until 1941, when a Joint Committee on Student Work was established. Under the able direction of Dr. Joseph M. Garrison, the first broad policies of work with students were formulated.

When the Presbyterian Church, U. S., was reorganized in 1950, the Joint Committee on Student Work became the Department of Campus Christian Life of the Board of Christian Education. This department "is directed by the General Assembly to lead and assist the whole Church in her ministry to all persons attending or teaching or working in colleges and universities within the bounds of the Assembly."[12]

The Department of Campus Christian Life has five main responsibilities:

1. Obtaining and training personnel. The ministry to the campus is presented to ordained ministers, students in seminaries and Assembly's Training School, and laymen in the professional and business worlds. A two-week seminar for new Campus Christian Life workers was held for the first time in Louisville, Kentucky, in June, 1955. It is the policy to call to the campus men and women who are mature, professional, mentally alert, and well-trained theologically.

2. Making available helpful material such as "The Campus Christian Life Manual," "Resource Materials for Westminster Fellowships," "Campus Christian Life News," Bible study materials, devotional booklets, and audio-visual materials.

3. Visits to campuses and counseling with the ministers to students, the local Campus Christian Life Committees, and the Westminster Fellowship Council.

4. Assisting the Synod's Campus Christian Life Committee when invited.

5. Co-operating with other denominational groups and participating in the ecumenical student movement.

## The Challenge to the Church: Providing Pastoral Care

Our ministry to the campus, guided by the Department of Campus Christian Life, is a challenge to the Church. Through this ministry, the Church has a part in the preaching of the Word of God, in providing pastoral care for all in the college community, and in training students and faculty as effective workers for Christ on the campus.

Tomorrow's leaders are in the classroom today. Who will make the laws and execute the functions of government? Who will develop new methods to heal sick bodies and minds? Who will build the homes of tomorrow? Who will go to the ends of the earth to proclaim the Good News of Jesus Christ? These questions are being answered by students every day. Here are our statesmen, our educators, our industrial and commercial leaders, our artists and philanthropists. Through the ministry of Campus Christian Life, the Presbyterian Church, U. S., is seeking to become a vital factor in the crucial decisions which students are making today.

## CHAPTER 7

*RENÉ de VISME WILLIAMSON*

Chairman and professor of government,
Louisiana State University, 1954—.

Ph.D., Harvard, 1935.

Elder, Presbyterian Church.

Chairman, Professors' Section, Presbyterian Educational Association of the
South, 1953-54.

Member, Executive Committee, Faculty
Christian Fellowship, 1953—.

Visited college campuses of South in
1953-54, promoting Faculty Christian
Fellowship movement.

Author, *Culture and Policy.*

Editor, *The Journal of Politics,* 1949-53

# Called to Witness

## FACULTY CHRISTIAN MOVEMENT

## *René de Visme Williamson*

### The Influence of the Professor

AN ELDERLY professor of psychology decided to dust the numerous books which lined the walls of his study and got his yardman to help him. After a while, this professor sat down in his comfortable leather armchair, lit his pipe, and settled down for a rest.

"It's a good thing, doctor," commented the yardman, "that you don't have to work for a livin'."

This remark epitomizes the curious mixture of respect and contempt which many people have for professors. American scholars are generally paid low salaries, make no profits, and are just about the only professional men whose offices may be visited by anyone free of charge. Deemed too impractical to be true laymen and yet not spiritual enough to be ministers, professors sometimes feel that they are threatened with the fate of that which is neither hot nor cold.

Nevertheless, there is some recognition of the important place which professors occupy in society. And well there might be! Professors create by experiment, research, and thought much of the knowledge and ideas, discoveries and inventions, which business and government use. Few people see what they do, but fewer still are unaffected by the consequences. Do you not believe it? Think of Karl Marx—once a professor—whose philosophy encompasses nearly half of the populated world. Think of the atomic scientists who have placed in our hands (or over our heads) the awesome power of nuclear energy!

Professors in state universities and church schools alike not only create knowledge: they teach it. They impart to each generation the cultural inheritance without which civilized living would cease to exist, and the skills that are necessary to professional success. By teaching, by writing books and articles, and by force of personal character, they do much to mold the values by which our college and university graduates live. I wonder if the average parent has any conception of how unique the teaching situation is. Most people can choose the books they want and are free to read them as carefully or carelessly as they like, or not at all. But the college student has no such freedom. His textbooks and most of his other books are chosen for him by his professors, and he will have to study them enough to pass examinations. Public lecturers, preachers, politicians, and radio commentators have large audiences, but these audiences are free. It is otherwise with professors. They have captive audiences. The students have to listen to the professors if they expect to pass their courses. Moreover, four years of close association with the faculty exerts a considerable extra-curricular influence on the students, because they are exposed not only to professional knowledge and skills, but also to personal attitudes, mannerisms, and outlooks on life.

In which direction and on whose behalf is this enormous weight of influence being exerted? This is a question of vital interest to every parent, present and prospective, of our college and university students. The Presbyterian Church, too, is profoundly interested in it not only for the sake of parent and student but for the sake of the professors themselves. The Board of Christian Education estimates that from five to six thousand professors in our Southern colleges and universities are Presbyterians, and many are elders and deacons in their local churches. This is an impressive number with a potential Christian influence that staggers the imagination. Who are these Presbyterian professors? Where are they? How distinguished are they professionally and in what fields? How strong and informed are they as Christians and how active are they as churchmen? Our Board of Christian Education is engaged in an extensive survey to gather this information.

## Handicaps of the Christian Professor

We can be sure that although we have grounds for hope as to the future, the results of this survey will be disappointing in some aspects. We could scarcely expect anything else when we stop to consider how overwhelmingly secularized American education has become. The great bulk of our youth now goes to the public schools and state universities in which teachers are chosen and promoted without regard to religious convictions; in which the claims of Christ are seldom presented in either lecture or textbook; and in which seldom is a place provided for reverence and worship. Many private educational institutions, once dedicated to the training of Christian ministers and Christian laymen, have long been severed from their original religious moorings. Even the remaining church-affiliated colleges and universities are affected by secularism, because their faculties are trained in graduate schools whose outlook is strongly secular, and because they are part of an America whose civilization has been dominated by pragmatism, utilitarianism, and materialism.

Secularism takes many forms, but the essence of all secularism is to leave God out of everything. It ignores the sovereignty of God over the universe; it deletes the Judeo-Christian tradition from the record of history and the face of the present; it has no place for sin or revelation or salvation; it pays no attention to the person and mission of Jesus Christ whose birth is the basis of the very calendar it uses. It strips all spiritual significance from the physical universe and all Christian values from human life, whether individual or social, in the name of objectivity. It interprets life in terms of geography, economics, technology, psychology, or almost anything else, so long as it is not religion. In short, secularism is either anti-Christian or non-Christian.

Consider now the plight of a professor who is a Christian. What is he going to use for a textbook? Suppose the best book on international relations is conceived in terms of the crassest power politics, eliminating all considerations of right and wrong. Should a political scientist require his students to buy it? Should a psychologist use as a textbook a work whose whole viewpoint is that man is an animal and nothing but an animal? What is a physicist to do who has a deep abiding sense of the glory and majesty of God's creation, if no acceptable textbook reflects even a glimmer of such a sense? Obviously, there is a painful tension in the Christian professor between the demands of his professional conscience, which impels him to abide by the judgment of the authorities in his field, and those of his Christian conscience which insists that he be true to his faith.

Consider again the predicament of the Christian professor who is peppered with student questions concerning religion. A political scientist is asked: "What is the difference between the classless society of Marx and the Kingdom of God?" He is professionally trained to answer the first part of the question, but he is tongue-tied on the second part because he doesn't know anything about the Kingdom of God. A geologist is asked: "Do you believe that God created the heavens and the earth and, if so, what evidence do you have for your belief?" The poor professor is in real trouble, because nowhere in his undergraduate and graduate work was the matter ever brought up. A philosopher is asked to compare Aristotelian with Christian ethics but, alas, he knows only the former. What is a professor to do about such questions as these? If he says, "I don't know," too often, it will undermine his authority; and he will be pricked by his conscience which tells him that he ought to know. If he gives ambiguous and evasive answers, his students will see through them. Truly, he is the victim of an incomplete and lopsided education.

As a result of this inadequate religious preparation the Christian professor frequently has taken refuge in a kind of professional isolationism. He has led one life in church and another on the campus, and the two lives have been kept separate to the detriment of both. Because he kept his intellectual activities confined to the campus, his religious knowledge and insights did not grow but remained pretty much what they were when he was an adolescent. His reading, research, and writing did not extend to his religion. He might love the Lord his God with all his heart, but not with all his strength—still less with all his mind. On the other hand, because he kept his religion confined to the church, he permitted anti-Christian professors to do all the talking about religion, his relations with students became official and narrow rather than personal and broad, and he lost a sense of community with his colleagues. Exceptions may be found, of course, in some staunch individuals who found places of teaching and leadership in the church along with their teaching. But they were in the minority.

## A New Spirit: The Faculty Christian Fellowship

At this point, mention must be made of the changing times in which we live. The climate of opinion in America is no longer what it was twenty years ago, and the change is reflected on college and university campuses. It is also reflected in professional societies. For example, at the 1953 meeting of the American Political Science Association, a paper was read on "The Latent Place of God in Twentieth Century Political Thought." This paper provoked a great deal of discussion, and for over half an hour, Protestant, Catholic, Jewish, humanist, and agnostic professors argued about what proofs we have of the existence of God, following which they debated the relationship between secularism and totalitarianism. Twenty years ago it would not have been academically respectable for the name of God to appear on the program of a great national professional society, and professors unaffiliated with the church would not have ventured into this kind of theological discussion.

There is a growing spiritual awakening in our American institutions of higher education which is becoming known as the faculty Christian movement. This movement is something which has sprung up spontaneously among scholars in our colleges and universities. It is to be found in all types of institutions, whether public, private, or denominational. It has adherents in small liberal arts colleges, large universities, graduate schools, technical institutes, and professional schools. It cuts across subject-matter disciplines and includes research and administrative personnel as well as faculty members in the narrower sense. It transcends sectional, denominational, and age limits. It is in its essence a reaction against an overwhelmingly secularized type of education and a rediscovery of the Gospel in an age of moral and ideological confusion. In short, it is a return, not merely to religion, but to Christianity itself.

To say that the faculty Christian movement has not made the headlines would be an understatement. Few people, even in academic circles, are aware of its existence. The reason is that the movement is still in its infancy. It still has to rid itself of the religious illiteracy which afflicts most of us, and to develop a solid and scholarly knowledge of the sources and grounds of the Christian faith—indeed, of the very nature and content of that faith. It is barely beginning to re-think subject-matter fields and professional relationships in terms of the Christian Gospel. It has to rediscover the roots of the Judeo-Christian tradition which underlie Western civilization and thus restore to academic knowledge that fullness of meaning which a dogmatic secularism has deleted from it. Only now is it beginning to develop organizations to serve its manifold purposes, express its growing convictions, and enable its members to become acquainted with one another.

Essentially, the faculty Christian movement is a response of scholars to the crisis of the age. We can no longer continue to regard peace as normal and war as abnormal when the notion of the cold war blurs the very distinction between war and peace and dooms us to the awful uncertainties of co-existence with Soviet imperialism for many years to come. The explosion of the atomic bomb at Hiroshima and the advent of loyalty checks and security investigations mean that there are no "safe" subjects any more, and that natural scientists must think through the moral responsibilities of technical knowledge and stand face to face with the spiritual significance of the physical universe. The failure of the social sciences to predict either the Great Depression or World War II, the involvement of social scientists in the field of government policy-making, the disillusionment over the efficacy of attaining the good life by government decree, and the conflicting and imperative demands of the so-called "isms" which hold the minds of men captive in ideological prisons have combined to force social scientists to reconsider the problems of values and the claims of personal commitment. The debates over education, progressive or otherwise, have brought a renewed concern about the goals of education. The concept of adjustment is losing some of its magic as thoughtful people perceive the dangers of interpreting individual adjustment to existing situations as conformity to imperfection, thereby jeopardizing the ability to criticize and to improve. The struggle over academic freedom has laid bare the underlying disunity in our university world with its chasms between faculty and students, faculty and administration, department and department.

These and many other developments have penetrated to the very heart of the campus. World-wide developments though they are, they have been brought to our own academic doorstep, toppling over our legendary ivory towers, and forcing their way into the laboratory, the office, and the classroom. They have come down to the personal level where the individual must make decisions.

Now many American scholars, one by one, in a multitude of ways, with faltering steps, have begun to inquire into the achievements and promises of their ancestral faith. They remember that co-existence is as old as the Christian Church; that the Scriptures teach the responsibilities of knowledge and delineate the spiritual foundations of all knowledge; that the same Messiah who came to make us free can liberalize our minds from the fetters of manmade philosophical systems which have split the world in two; that the New Testament is the authority on how a man can accommodate himself to this world even at its worst and yet remain untainted by it. Why not, these scholars asked themselves, explore this forgotten portion of our cultural inheritance? Why should the claims of the Christian religion be the only ones that we do not investigate, analyze, and put to the test of experiment, if not of experience?

Faculty response has taken numerous forms. Many of them have been on a strictly individual plane. Some professors have done a great deal of reading and thinking whose fruits are appearing as books dealing with Christianity and education. Others have obtained grants from foundations and have gone to leading seminaries for a year's study of theology. Still others have incorporated Christian insights in the courses they taught and quietly restored the Christian content of literary masterpieces and social institutions which their creators had put there.

There has also been an increasing response from college and university administrators. Departments of religion have been established in state universities, such as the University of North Carolina. At the University of Tennessee there is an autonomous School of Religion in which leading Knoxville ministers offer, on the campus, courses which are acceptable for credit toward academic degrees. The University of Arkansas has developed an integrated course whose common core is values, taught co-operatively by members of five departments. The University of Texas and Austin Theological Seminary co-operate in a program in Christian education leading to the master's degree. Denominational institutions like Emory have developed programs, both undergraduate and graduate, in which Christian theology is integrated with other fields. Other denominational institutions, like Davidson, have established a permanent faculty committee to study the whole meaning of a Christian college, to the end that Christian higher education shall be more than just the usual secularized curriculum with an appendage of Bible courses and extra-curricular Christian trimmings.

As faculty members became engaged in these new programs, they soon realized that they were operating on a very slim theological foundation. They whose whole professional outlook stressed the importance of training and background discovered that they lacked the kind of foundation which they consider indispensable in their own fields of professional competence. They were unfamiliar with the Bible, knew little about the teachings of the churches to which they belonged, and were ignorant of theology and current theological literature. How could they impart to students that which they did not themselves possess? It was a case of teacher, teach thyself.

Another problem arose from the desire to retain what is best in modern secular scholarship. These Christian professors were anxious to maintain their traditional academic respect for facts, logic, and relevance. They asked: Can you bring your Christian faith into your subject without wandering off from that subject? Can you reconcile personal Christian commitment with a fair presentation of non-Christian doctrines and attitudes? Can you experience a new sense of responsibility that should go with the teaching of youth, and still exemplify a scrupulous respect for the right of students to think for themselves and arrive at their own conclusions?

It was inevitable that, as professors grappled with these twin problems of becoming theologically literate and of relating their growing theological knowledge to their fields, they should turn to each other for help. The result was the formation of small faculty study and discussion groups on many campuses. These groups were completely informal gatherings without organization, constitutions, minutes, or dues. Sometimes they met for lunch at some convenient place, at other times in faculty homes for an evening session. One of the most successful and lasting of such groups is the so-called Philosophy Club of Mississippi State College where twelve professors, meeting once every two weeks over a period of five years, have put themselves through a stiff course of study in Christian ethics and theology. Another successful group is at Vassar, where twenty faculty members have met twice a month to make an intensive study of the New Testament. At the University of Tennessee an average of fifty Presbyterian professors have met once a month for two years to discuss the relationship of their faith to their professional life and fields. Different members present papers drawing on their own resources and experience and embodying the best of their thinking as of that time.

In general it may be said that these local campus groups were the product of local initiative and that, quite literally, they operated as the Spirit moved them. They lived without benefit of outside stimulation, without a well-planned program of study, without experienced leadership. As a result, they appeared, disappeared, and re-appeared. They had to fight for a place in the busy lives of professors who have somehow or other to satisfy the claims of home life, research activities, teaching duties, committee work, and professional societies. Nevertheless, the achievements of these groups were considerable. Thought was stimulated, the stock of information was enlarged, departmental barriers and prejudices were lowered or altogether eliminated. It often happened that faculty members, who had known one another only on the personal and social levels, became acquainted for the first time as intellectuals and scholars, so that professional respect was added to personal friendship.

As was to be expected, faculty concern for the Christian religion and its implications for education could not be confined to individual campuses considered as small isolated universes. No Christian movement could remain intra-mural. It was destined to be intercollegiate, national, and even international.

The wider inter-campus needs of the faculty Christian movement are being met partially by two types of gatherings: the consultation and the conference. The consultation is usually the smaller of the two and is concerned with planning, program-making, and finances. It is a necessary, though often frustrating, activity because it skirts around or leaves out the substantive discussion of the concerns which are its *raison d'être*. As the word consultation implies, various non-faculty people such as officials from denominational boards and the National Council of Churches are invited to meet with the professors and give them the benefit of their experience and insights. The conference, on the other hand, deals directly with the problems which have brought the faculty Christian movement into existence and is attended almost entirely by professors.

The Faculty Christian Fellowship was formed in October, 1952, at Berea, Kentucky. It is an association, nation-wide in scope, of

Christian professors working together on a non-denominational basis. It is difficult to characterize the nature of this association because of the complexity of its desires and because it is still in its formative stage. It is definitely not a federation of denominational movements, although it co-operates with them. Neither is it an organization of non-denominational movements; it regards itself as a single whole. It encourages and promotes local campus fellowships but does not regard them as chapters. It has no regional organs. Only in November of 1954 did it decide to have membership dues, but the phrase "membership dues" is misleading. It has "Fellows" rather than members; the contributions are not called "dues" and the amount is not a fixed one, and the reasons for having dues at all are more psychological than financial.

At present the Faculty Christian Fellowship may best be described as the national staff and liaison agency of the faculty Christian movement. It has an Executive Committee, an editor who is responsible for the publication of *The Christian Scholar*, and an executive director. The Executive Committee is assisted by a Board of Consultants which is a kind of panel of non-faculty people nominated by the Church boards, foundations, and other non-university bodies interested in Christian higher education. The financial and administrative aspects of the Faculty Christian Fellowship are handled by the Department of Campus Christian Life of the National Council of Churches.

The Faculty Christian Fellowship has held one national conference at Park College, Missouri, in June, 1953, and numerous consultations. It has also sponsored or participated in many regional faculty conferences. It publishes an excellent magazine, *The Christian Scholar*, which is an outlet for the thinking of Christian professors, a source of intellectual stimulation for the faculty Christian movement as a whole, and a medium of information about activities and publications of interest to its readers. It has published and is revising a very fine classified and annotated bibliography and a *Manual* for the use of local groups. Its executive director, Professor J. Edward Dirks, who was on leave of absence from Lake Forest College for two years, has traveled from coast to coast stimulating interest in the faculty Christian movement in American colleges and universities and promoting local campus fellowships.

## Presbyterian Faculty Movement

In spite of its national scope and its outstanding achievements, the Faculty Christian Fellowship is far from being the only form through which the faculty Christian movement is expressed. There are many Christian professors for whom a denominational connection is meaningful and precious. They have a strong feeling for the rich and unique heritage of their Church and they want to explore that heritage. They consider that they are a part and parcel of the Church, through which they are never without direct channels for all kinds of assistance. Through the Church they have immediate access to seminaries and denominational boards, and have a natural anchor wherever they go. They want their Christian growth as professors to be expressed in, and organically related to, the work of the Church. This point of view is especially strong among the Presbyterians of the South, and among the Episcopalians, and has found fulfillment in two distinct faculty movements. Let it be noted, however, that these movements are in no way opposed to the Faculty Christian Fellowship. On the contrary, they work with it on all levels and consider themselves part of it.

The National Council of Churches is not the only church organization interested in the faculty Christian movement. Our own Presbyterian Church in the United States has long been concerned with its faculty members and is giving them powerful and growing support. The Presbyterian Educational Association of the South was founded as far back as 1913, and has been one of the several evidences of the Church's sense of responsibility in the field of education. In 1947 the Association added a fourth section, the Faculty or Professors' Section, to give specific recognition to the spiritual awakening on our campuses.

For several years the Annual Educational Conference at Montreat was something of a flickering light in so far as the Presbyterian faculty movement was concerned. It consisted of a small group of professors, numbering from 25 to 30, most of whom came from the immediate Southeastern states. It was held in the middle of June, an unpropitious time for faculty people since it conflicted with commencement or summer school. In 1953 the Executive Committee and the Board representatives met at Clemson, South Carolina, and made elaborate plans to develop not merely the Montreat Conference but the Presbyterian faculty movement as a whole. The plans were discussed and ratified at Montreat at its 1953 meeting. The year 1954 saw a much enlarged conference at Montreat of more than 100 professors, meeting jointly with Methodist professors for a period of five days. Mornings were devoted to theology, afternoons to academic fields in relation to the Christian religion, and evenings to a general survey of trends affecting the Church in a world-wide sense. The conference of 1955 was planned following the pattern set in 1954, except that the date was moved to late August.

The Board of Christian Education has taken vigorous steps to encourage the emerging faculty Christian movement. One of these was to help professors in holding regional faculty conferences on religion and education. Since 1952 several such conferences have been held at the University of Tennessee, at the Texas Agricultural and Mechanical College, and at Mississippi State College. These conferences usually take place on week ends and are built around three papers and a special worship service. Many more such conferences are being planned.

The effects of these regional conferences are not confined to intellectual stimulation. At the 1953 conference in Knoxville, what stood out was not the quality of the papers presented, high though that was. More striking was a general amazement at the fact of Christian fellowship. It was discovered that there were 150 Presbyterians on the faculty of the University of Tennessee. Nor was it merely the number that was impressive. Among those present were many of the intellectually most distinguished, professionally most influential, and personally most eminent members of the Tennessee faculty and administration. These men and women, who had known each other for years, were completely unaware of the extent of their activities in Knoxville's many

Presbyterian churches. One could see surprise lighting up one face after another. These professors had suddenly realized that they were not little isolated lights flickering in a vast secular darkness but a mighty company of Christian scholars and teachers. The common delusion, shared alike by faculty and students, that they stand alone in their Christian faith, was dispelled in one moment and replaced by a thrilling sense of community. The spiritual momentum which was thus generated survived the summer months and led to the establishment of one of the strongest faculty groups in the South.

Regional conferences also serve another very important purpose: they break down the barriers and prejudices which separate professors into groups—which make the modern university look like an academic landscape strewn with human fragments, instead of the orderly and harmonious community it was intended to be.

The Board of Christian Education is strengthening the faculty Christian movement at the grass-roots level by organizing local faculty groups dedicated to the serious study of the Christian faith and the systematic discussion of the meaning of that faith for professors. In 1954 it sent out a professor, who had obtained leave of absence from his institution, to visit colleges and universities all over the South for the purpose of acquainting faculty people with the faculty Christian movement and assisting them in organizing local groups. This venture resulted in an anonymous gift of $25,000 to the Board to step up its faculty work. This gift enables the Board to assist some professors from the more distant colleges and universities to attend the Faculty Conference on Religion and Education. Through the grant the Board of Christian Education in co-operation with the Presbyterian professors' group also is sending each year another professor on circuit to visit institutions of higher learning in the South. In addition two more professors will go to foreign universities, one in Latin America and one in Asia.

The faculty Christian movement is a typically Protestant phenomenon. This does not imply antagonism toward Catholicism, for Catholic professors have participated in some local campus groups and would be given a place in the Faculty Christian Fellowship leadership if they wanted it. Its structure is Protestant in that it achieves unity without uniformity and co-operation without subordination. It is Protestant in its adherence to the Bible as the standard of thought and practice, and in its faith in the Holy Spirit as the all-sufficient source of power and light to give the movement the necessary central direction. It is Protestant in its emphasis on the Christian vocation of every man—including professors. And its Protestantism is of the most admirable kind in that it is so free of negativism in a world which is so full of it, for the Fellowship looks upon Catholics with respect and good will as fellow Christians to whom all of us are indebted; upon the Jews as kinfolk who, by the Providence of God, gave us our Bible and our Christ; and upon Christians in other nations and continents as brothers in one great ecumenical fellowship.

The faculty Christian movement will mean much to American higher education. It will lead to the writing of papers, articles, monographs, treatises, and textbooks. Thus will grow a new literary output written in response not to the private ambitions of individual scholars, nor to the pressure of university administrations, but to the same Christian urge that built our cathedrals and inspired some of our finest music. It will reverse the centrifugal character of much contemporary knowledge and impart to it a measure of integration. It will restore to our colleges and universities a long-lost sense of organic oneness, because it will supply a common meeting ground and center of interest, a common channel of communication, and a common body of Christian experience and language by means of which instructional and administrative staffs can be brought together. Professors will lose their separatism which so often makes them poor academic citizens, and will gain an infinitely greater concern for students as individual human beings with a Christian destiny to fulfill, which will give new life and force to teaching.

The Christian professors of this country are experiencing a real call to witness and are responding to it.

## DENISON MAURICE ALLAN

Professor of philosophy and psychology, Hampden-Sydney College, Hampden-Sydney, Va., 1923—.

A.B. and M.A., Hampden-Sydney College. Ph.D., Harvard, 1926.

Director, Presbyterian Guidance Center, Hampden-Sydney College.

Author, *The Realm of Personality.*

Contributor to journals of philosophy and psychology.

## DALLAS H. SMITH

Director, Department of Christian Vocation, Board of Christian Education, of Presbyterian Church (U.S.), 1951—.

Majored in personnel administration and labor problems at Johns Hopkins University, University of Maryland, and University of Alabama.

Deacon, elder, and church school teacher in Presbyterian Church.

Member, American Personnel and Guidance Association; National Vocational Guidance Association; Administrative Committee, Department of Ministry, Joint Department of Christian Vocation, National Council of Churches.

Experience: Personnel manager, Montgomery Ward & Company; Director of Industrial and Public Relations, Ingalls' Shipbuilding Corporation; Director of Industrial Relations, Capital Airlines, Inc.; general superintendent, J. B. Ivey & Co.

Former president, Washington, D. C., Personnel Association; former member, Board of Governors, American Public Relations Association.

# Serving God Through Lifework

## PRESBYTERIAN GUIDANCE PROGRAM

## D. Maurice Allan
## Dallas H. Smith

SOMETIME in every person's life he must face the question: "What shall I choose for my life's work?" The decision may spell happiness or unhappiness, a useful career or a life of frustration. For in choosing a vocation one chooses not merely the manner in which he will spend eight hours a day, but the kind of service which he will render to society and the kind of world in which he will rear his children.

What factors influenced your choice? Was it the urging of your parents, or the example of some friend, or a job opportunity that happened your way? What motives will influence the choice of your son or daughter?

Today the young person who faces this choice has a more difficult decision to make than his father or grandfather. The reasons are plain:

1. The increasing specialization and complexity of society have multiplied the variety of jobs from which choices are to be made. More than 22,000 different job categories were listed in the *Dictionary of Occupational Titles* when it was printed in 1949.

2. Many of the more promising vocations have become highly technical and require a long and expensive education. The choice of such a vocation involves many related decisions about time, money, and personal relations.

3. The rising standard of living has accustomed many of our young people to luxuries that are costly to maintain; therefore pressure is exerted to choose vocations on a basis of financial reward. A promising college senior remarked not long ago: "The choice between teaching and a business career is a hard one for me. I would like to teach, but I came from a poor home. I don't want my children to endure such privation as I knew." The business world offered him twice as much to start with, and he accepted.

4. Personal hazards complicate choices in many areas of work. Many jobs produce tensions and strains, physical or mental or emotional. Occupational injuries cost the nation over two and a half billion dollars and take the lives of about 18,000 workers each year. Among administrative employees, and in sales organizations, the competition is so intense that many men and women develop ulcers, insomnia, hypertension, and nervous irritability. In many jobs uncertainty of tenure heightens tension and frustration.

5. A person of high Christian standards faces problems in avoiding jobs in which he will be called upon to do something contrary to his integrity. Many men in business and industry feel compelled by competition to engage in unfair practices. Shoddy materials and unsafe structures often escape the attention of inspectors. Some business contracts are secured with the aid of secret bonuses and indecent carousals. Certain types of journalism flourish by featuring crime, obscenity, and the blasting of reputations. Investments of capital in foreign lands may be for exploitation rather than for constructive development. Even educational institutions may compete shamelessly for students, faculty, and athletes.

## The Vocational Misfit: A Grave Social Problem

The making of the right vocational choice has consequences that go far beyond the individual. It affects the family, the community, and society as a whole. In a certain five-year period over thirty-three million persons seeking employment were registered with the United States Employment Service. About eight million were young people from sixteen to twenty-five years of age with little or no work experience. A larger number were older workers who had been turned away or displaced from industry for one cause or another. In many employment areas the turnover is large and the cost of training new workers is heavy for both employer and the public.

But these financial costs are hardly to be compared to the human cost in failure, frustration, and heartbreak. Scientifically conducted polls have indicated that at least two fifths of all employed workers are unhappy in their work. Had they to do it all over again, they would choose another occupation. The greater part of this dissatisfaction is due to the fact that most workers did not know how to find out what they were really fitted to do. The longer the training required, the deeper the frustration if a wrong choice has been made. Every vocational counselor comes to know men in their thirties or forties who realize that they have made a dreadful mistake. But having families to support, they feel that launching upon a new career is too hazardous an undertaking.

It has been demonstrated that parental example, the advice of friends, job opportunities available, and the lure of "big money" are all unsound criteria for selecting one's lifework. In one study cited by Dr. Donald E. Super, one of the foremost authorities on vocational guidance in this country, two thirds of those who chose their vocation for financial reasons were unhappy. While following in father's footsteps may sometimes be wise, there is often a basic difference of aptitudes and personality between parents and children. Many parents inadvisedly try to push their sons and daughters into vocational avenues which are not really suited to them.

A certain dentist who had desired to be a surgeon projected his disappointed hopes onto his only son. The boy dragged through one pre-medical course after another until he began to show symptoms of a nervous breakdown. The father was wise enough then to withdraw all pressures and allow his son to prepare for what he really wanted to be—a journalist.

Where both parents are involved, the conflict may be even more severe. The writer had occasion to counsel a distraught college student whose dominant desire was to become an artist. His mother wished him to be a teacher. His father, who was an engineer, felt nothing but contempt for artists. Only after the unhappy youth passed through a serious mental crisis did his parents relent and send him to an art school where he was later reported to be happy and doing well.

## The Right Basis for Choices

It is our conviction that the right choice of a lifework is determined by the harmonious relationship of three factors: (1) the person's discovery of God's will for his life; (2) his peculiar combination of abilities, interests, and personality traits; and (3) society's need for such skills and assets. When this right relationship is not found, the result is unhappiness, and often a squandered life.

A rising young businessman came to a Presbyterian Guidance Center. His income was more than adequate. He had money in the bank. He was happily married and the proud father of three fine children. He was active in church and community. The sun seemed to shine upon him. Yet deep down in his heart he was profoundly dissatisfied. It turned out that he was in a ruthlessly competitive business whose harsh demands were in constant conflict with his social conscience. This irresolvable conflict was robbing him of peace of mind. Because he had grown accustomed to a certain standard of living, and because in many ways he enjoyed his work, this young man was faced with a very difficult choice.

In sharp contrast to this is the case of a young man known to the writer who, having inherited a modest fortune, had the vocational problem of deciding how to invest his capital as well as his energies. He had come to realize that the life of the idle rich is futile and boring. One day, while still in perplexity, he came across a ragged and dirty newsboy in one of the slum neighborhoods of the city in which he lived. On an impulse he took the boy home to his luxurious apartment. His guest was starry-eyed, for he had known nothing but a filthy tenement. During the night this young man began to do some thinking and toward morning he reached a decision. As a result he invested his money in a home and industrial institute for poor city boys. Later he added a farm in the country and a recreational center in the heart of the slums. In order to do this he had to live quite simply. One night he took the writer to a swimming pool that he had just built. Soon we were sitting on the edge watching a score of naked boys as they splashed and yelled to their heart's content. He contemplated their antics with kindly interest, then turned and said, "You can't help loving these kids. I seldom have one that doesn't turn out well. I can't imagine a job that would have given me half so much satisfaction."

This story conveys the essence of what we mean by "Christian vocation." Here was a man of culture and substantial means, with some natural talent for leadership and planning. He might have gone far in the business world and, conceivably, this might have been God's call to him. But he saw a need and he saw his talents and resources in relation to that need. Out of his kind heart, his clear mind, and his Christian conscience, there came to him a vocation to which he gave of his best and was happy.

We should not infer, however, that a social service occupation is intrinsically superior or more Christian than business or engineering or flying a plane. Each of these vocations requires aptitudes so distinctive and so specialized that a young person who is endowed with them is in a position to render a far greater service to society than one who is ever so well-meaning but lacks the requisite abilities.

Many boys and girls, especially among our college youth, want to enter one of the "learned professions" because of their greater prestige, and hence reject the humbler but equally necessary callings. Society needs farmers, telephone linemen, bench chemists, bookkeepers, and country school teachers. A boy who would like to be a corporation lawyer might be more useful as a pharmacist, and a girl who aspires to be an airline hostess might be happier as a small town stenographer.

It is best for us to abandon false standards of rating occupations in terms of money or prestige, and to think primarily of the kind of service rendered and the degree of responsibility undertaken. Too many of our college graduates come forth into the world feeling that they merit opportunities that other young men and women do not, and that hard toil will not be needed. It is true that a young person with a well-trained mind may go farther. But he should think of his educational advantage not as a priority but as an obligation, not as a personal privilege but as a moral challenge. To combat the sordidness, the banality, and the selfish striving that pervade so many secular callings, the highest type of leadership from our college graduates is urgently needed.

## The Church's Concern About Vocational Choice

What is the stake of the Church in youth's choice of a lifework? It is twofold. The first point is that true religion is most vitally concerned with our deepest human needs and our most momentous decisions. If the Church cannot help young people in what is central in their lives, it will soon find itself on the periphery. Vocational choice for each young person is definitely tied up with the whole meaning and purpose of life.

The second point is that one's lifework is not only an opportunity for service to mankind, but also a means of Christian witness. The Reformers, notably Luther and Calvin, upheld the basically Scriptural view that every man and woman is called of God to serve through his secular work, just as truly as through his walk and conversation at other times. The servant in the kitchen is serving God and human need just as usefully and honorably as the minister in the pulpit. The primary question that confronts each Christian is not "How important shall my service be?" but, "In what sphere of work does God have need of my energies and talents?"

In our generation the Church has caught a new vision of what a vital sense of Christian vocation may mean in the transformation of individuals and society. This may come about in three ways: (1) the superior quality of our work when regarded as an expression of love to God and gratitude for His gifts of mind, heart, and skill; (2) the spirit of generosity and devotion that shines through the Christian's work, commending his life to others; and (3) the lively concern of every true Christian to help create more just, humane, and upright standards of conduct within his secular calling. This cannot be limited to drawing up codes of professional and business ethics or assenting to them. For even where such codes are professed, many cynical, dishonest, and unfair practices prevail. Think of what it would mean if the attorney in the courtroom put justice and mercy above the winning of the case; if the businessman rejected every shady deal and considered service above profits; if the teacher treated the failing pupil not as a dead loss to be shrugged off but as a precious potential to be reclaimed; or if the physician were passionately concerned about ending the inequalities of medical service.

But what of the Ford employee who puts three bolts in every car body on the assembly line? Can the ministry of daily work mean anything for him? Yes, if he tightens each bolt to the correct degree, if he is friendly and cheerful, if he helps his fellow workers on and off the job, if he refrains from cursing and bad temper, if he stands up for the right kind of labor union.

The supreme importance of such a sense of mission in all vocations is, that if it were really put into practice, it would carry the spirit of Christ far out into the crossways of the world—into its farms, factories, stores, hospitals, classrooms, and shipyards. But this dream will not become a reality unless we make it central in the lives of our young people in their formative stages. How can this be done?

## What the Church Is Doing About It

By the action of the 1949 General Assembly, the Presbyterian Church in the United States provided for a Department of Christian Vocation in the Board of Christian Education. In 1951, plans were made to realize this ideal. Lexington Presbytery, through its pioneer vocational guidance center at Fishersville, Virginia, had already shown the tremendous possibilities of this approach. Through the co-operation of leaders of local churches, presbyteries, and synods, and through the initiative of the church-related colleges in which they were established, six additional Presbyterian Guidance Centers were put into operation by 1955.* Similar centers are in process of development, and the original center at Fishersville has been moved to Mary Baldwin College in Staunton, Virginia. There, with a larger staff, the center will expand its services to serve not only Lexington Presbytery youth but also those of three other presbyteries in the synod as well as the students of Mary Baldwin.

*"Abilities, opportunities, time, life, are the gifts of God."*
*Presbyterian guidance counselor helps student plan use of talents*
*with a sense of stewardship.*

Each of these centers is under the direction of a trained counseling psychologist, and is equipped with standard, up-to-date testing materials. High school students in the junior and senior years, as well as college students, are given two days of testing and counseling at these centers, by appointment. This service is

* Flora Macdonald, Hampden-Sydney, Centre, Presbyterian, Davis and Elkins, Southwestern at Memphis.

without charge to the counselee and is equally available to those who do not expect to go to college.

Some of the centers are scheduled for months ahead with appointments for testing and counseling. Many young people come from distances of one hundred to three hundred miles to avail themselves of this opportunity, and in such cases they may spend the night so as to be in residence for two whole days. Those who come from shorter distances frequently return for the second day after an interval of a week or more.

It is expected that each young person who visits one of our Presbyterian Guidance Centers will come with a clear understanding of the underlying philosophy of Christian vocation. In order that he may get maximum help from this counseling experience, he should know what vocational guidance is and how it can aid him in his search for the work for which he has both opportunity and talent. To point this up in the local church, the Department of Christian Vocation has issued a manual outlining the Presbyterian Guidance Program, how it can be set up in each local church, and how the Sunday school teacher, Youth Fellowship adviser, and the vocational aide can work together to help each youth secure full benefit from the Program.

The "vocational aides" are volunteer leaders in the local churches' part of the Presbyterian Guidance Program. Efforts have been made to enlist those who can work effectively with young people. Many who have become outstanding aides had never before responded to the call for leadership in their churches but welcomed this opportunity. They have been school teachers, personnel directors, employment managers, social service workers, business and professional men and women, and parents.

Sunday school lessons and Youth Fellowship program materials for Junior and Senior High youth already emphasize that Christian witness through lifework is an integral part of commitment to Christ. To this is added additional literature on Christian vocation for both youth and leaders, along with study booklets which help prepare each young person to plan his career wisely. These are studied and reviewed in personal interviews with the vocational aide. All this literature is contained in a "Pre-Vocational Guidance Kit" and is available to every local church at a reasonable cost.*

In addition to helping prepare each young person to make the most of his guidance opportunity at the Center, the vocational aide also assists in leading discussions in youth meetings to help young people think out their lifework in terms of Christian service and dedication of talents. Personal interviews continue this emphasis.

Ideally, the young person begins this training period in his second year of high school and visits the Guidance Center in his third or fourth year. His appointment is made by the vocational aide, who also sends helpful information about him to the Center counselor, and arranges for his grades and psychological test data to be forwarded directly from his high school counselor. All this is tremendously helpful to the Center psychologist and enables him to do more effective counseling and testing with much saving of time. In return, the Guidance Center sends to the school counselor and to the vocational aide in the church such counseling data on each student as may be helpful in his further guidance.

## The Process of Christian Vocational Counseling

Let us visit one of our Guidance Centers and see what goes on. It is a Saturday morning. Two high school seniors, Jack Evans and Charlene Harris, have arrived at the Center. Appointments were made for them about two months ago by their vocational aide in their local church. Their high school records, and a questionnaire about their hobbies, activities, favorite studies, job experiences, and family backgrounds, have already been sent in.

In preliminary interviews the vocational counselor encourages them to tell of their plans or perplexities about their choices of lifework. Then they are ushered into the testing room and the serious work begins. First they are given one or two "vocational interest tests." The scoring of these reveals to the counselor that Jack is keenly interested in mechanical and scientific affairs, in all sorts of mathematical calculation, and to a lesser extent in artistic

---

* From Presbyterian Book Stores in Atlanta, Dallas, and Richmond.

things. All this is quite consistent with Jack's expressed interest in chemical engineering. But will he demonstrate the abilities to back up his interest pattern? Charlene shows that she has strong literary,

*Presbyterian Guidance Centers use standardized psychological tests.*

musical, and social service interests and that she is above average in outdoor and in scientific interest. She is not sure what she wants to be but feels that she would like to work with people. As the counselor observes her friendly and rather outspoken personality, he thinks to himself that she might well fit into some social welfare occupation. Will she have the aptitudes to match? We shall see.

Jack and Charlene are then given "intelligence tests" which probe their problem-solving ability and their capacity for dealing with abstract principles. Both are well above average with IQ's of 120 and 130 respectively. It is probable that Jack will have to work harder than Charlene to attain success in college work. As to their high school background, further tests indicate that Jack has a superior knowledge of math and science and that he is somewhat weak in English. Charlene is high in English and social studies, has a fair knowledge of science, and is at least average in mathematics.

After lunch in the college dining hall, Jack and Charlene undergo a series of "aptitude tests." These are designed to measure ability to profit by training along special lines, and thus indicate future potentiality rather than present knowledge. Jack does very well in tests with mechanical comprehension, space relations, computation, and design judgment. He also does well in manual tests in which he has to fit variously shaped blocks into appropriate holes or in which he must manipulate tools, screws, and bolts. Charlene does extremely well in so-called tests of "social intelligence" or "personal-social aptitude." She is also high in "judgment and comprehension" and in "expression" or facility in English usage. Her musical ability and art ability are above average but not outstanding.

Jack and Charlene have now put in a good day's work and say good-by to return the next Saturday. On the appointed morning they take a reading test which reveals that Charlene is a quick reader and comprehends well what she reads. She also has an excellent vocabulary. Jack is a much slower reader but has a fairly good technical vocabulary and is good at reading maps, tables, and graphs. Personality traits are now tested by means of so-called "personality inventories" and "attitude scales." Jack may be described as a careful, deliberate, reflective person who is friendly on the surface but not sociable or warm in personal relationships. Charlene is very friendly, enthusiastic, co-operative, emotionally stable, and ready to take the initiative. The church is vital to her existence and beyond that the world of human relationships is most real. Jack's values are technical and economic and next to these comes the religious side of life.

When the testing is over the counselor interviews Jack and Charlene separately and tries to help them reach a clearer understanding of themselves in the light of the test results and of their school records and activities. His task is not to tell them specifically what to do with their lives, but rather to make clear to them the most promising alternatives from among which they must reach their own decisions. So Jack may reasonably consider chemical or electrical engineering, scientific research, science teaching, and architecture. The pros and cons must be weighed. Is he, for example, interested enough in people to make a good teacher? Does he have enough initiative and planning ability to conduct scientific research? Charlene gives definite promise in such vocations as director of Christian education, home or foreign missionary, and English teacher. Yet her interests and her personality are not fully developed. It is possible that as she goes through college, her latent interest in social work may become dominant. At present her desire to be a director of Christian education seems fitting and worthy to be encouraged.

In this final interview the counselor should not shrink from pointing out any weak points or unrealized potentials which might be handicaps. Jack should take steps to improve his reading ability and to learn how to be genuinely friendly. Charlene is perhaps too impulsive and her impetuosity, though refreshing, may lead her into difficulties.

The counselor's final task in his closing interview and also by follow-up letter is to give Jack and Charlene helpful clues on how to make the right decision. To seek God's will through earnest prayer; to make a firsthand study of each of the vocations under consideration by observation, reading, and discussion; to ascertain the existing need (some vocations are overcrowded, others desperately short of competent applicants); and to plan carefully the right kind of training for each vocational choice and to consider how it can be financed—these are the steps that should be taken. The question to be faced and answered is, "In what avenue of service to my fellow men can God best use the aptitudes and endowments which He has given me and how can I best prepare myself to make this unique contribution to the life of my time?"

## Guidance Centers in Church Colleges

Why has the church college been chosen as the place to establish a guidance center? There are many reasons for this decision. First, it is essential that the vocational psychologist who undertakes so great a responsibility shall himself be one whose Christian faith enables him to see that the capacity to serve one's fellows, through right relationship to God, is fundamental to right choice. Second, the church-related college is likely to have one or more Christian psychologists on its staff, and an administration with a similarly Christian vision of the college's responsibility for the guidance of its own students. Third, a vocational counselor in a church college should be fully informed about vocational opportunities in church work, and thus can explain such possibilities to interested young people. A fourth reason is that young people of promise who visit the guidance center for testing and interviewing are given an opportunity to become acquainted with their own synod's college and its educational advantages.

What of thousands of Presbyterian students on the campuses of state universities and other secular institutions? These have the opportunity to visit a Presbyterian Guidance Center before they enter the college of their choice, or they may still do so during their vacations.

To meet the needs of these youth, the Department of Campus Christian Life in co-operation with the Department of Christian Vocation has made available to ministers to students a "Pre-Vocational Guidance Kit" on the college and university level. Members of campus Westminster Fellowships will thus be encouraged to make greater use of these Centers, and also to utilize to the fullest the guidance resources available to them in the state or private institutions they attend. In all such orientation programs there should be highlighted the need for consecrated, highly trained leadership in the Church, in business and industry, in the professions, and in public life.

## A Look to the Future

The Presbyterian Church, U. S., has made an encouraging beginning in this great enterprise of enlisting the capacities of youth in the service of Christ through their vocations. Six or seven hundred of our young people have already availed themselves of the complete guidance program. Before this program can be made a reality within the whole area served by our Church, many costly steps must be taken. In synods where the distances are great, more than one Guidance Center will undoubtedly be needed. To obtain properly trained personnel for these Centers and to finance them adequately so that they can render an efficient service, great wisdom and much consecrated effort will be necessary.

Moreover, all adults must bear the responsibility of creating in the minds of youth a willingness to approach any lifework as a task of Christian commitment. How can the lure of the immediate and the blandishments of selfish advantage be made to give way to human compassion and the unobtrusive things of the spirit in this basic choice?

First, we need a clear philosophy of Christian vocation. The major premise of this is that God is at work in the world, creatively and redemptively. The minor premise is that the Creator who has given us every talent and every grace that we possess *has a significant place for each of us in the unfolding of His universal plan.*

Second, we need to make this Christian concept of work a living reality in the home. Boys and girls do not first start to work when they get their first job baby-sitting or working in a department store at Christmas time. Long before that, they are entrusted with little services in the home, small errands, and larger responsibilities. Then comes school with its irksome restraints but unfolding opportunities of development and community living from the first day of the first grade to the last day of college. Will the child learn in the home and in school the secret of being happy through giving one's best to *every* task, however uninviting?

Christian higher education, likewise, must bear much of the responsibility to make this vision of a totally dedicated life service both appealing and challenging to college young people. At least a third of them have not found a worth-while goal. A majority have not begun to think seriously of their *Christian vocation as students.* For being a student is just as truly a divine calling as being a lawyer, physician, or teacher. The young person who has really understood his Christian vocation as a student will not be one-sided. He will realize the great value of the social life and the extra-curricular activities on the campus for developing the total person. Yet hard and faithful study will be a *must*, for a fully committed Christian knows that in the world of today God wants clear-thinking, well-informed, disciplined minds.

Christian colleges and tax-supported institutions alike must provide an alert, co-operative relationship between deans, faculty advisers, and the college counseling service, to salvage those students who are unhappily drifting.

Finally, it is of the utmost importance that every college teacher, administrator, athletic coach, and counselor should find his own Christian vocation. To impart this vision to faculty members is one of the great aims of the Faculty Christian Movement* which is gaining momentum in this country and whose future holds great promise for church and nation. One thinks of Thomas Hill Green, whose idealistic teachings inspired a generation of British students at Oxford with the idea of self-realization through service to state and community. Henry Drummond not only interpreted biology from a Christian point of view but was an attractive spiritual force on every campus that he visited. Arthur Latham Perry, beloved professor of economics at Williams College, challenged his students' minds and touched their hearts with his warm personal interest. Almost every campus has such men as these who, unheralded and with little hope of reward, live out their days as servants of truth and as quickeners of the creative spirit.

The Church will show true statesmanship to the extent that it nurtures, recruits, and encourages those who as teachers and guides of youth will confront their students with the living reality of Christian vocation in action.

---

* See Chapter 7.

## CHAPTER 9

## HUNTER BRYSON BLAKELY, JR.

Secretary, Division of Higher Education, Board of Christian Education, Presbyterian Church (U.S.), 1950—.

Graduate, Princeton Theological Seminary, 1919. Princeton Fellow to University of Edinburgh, 1921-22. Student at Oxford University in England, 1927, and University of Berlin, 1927-28.

Pastor, Presbyterian churches in Louisville and Harrodsburg, Ky., and Staunton, Va., and acting pastor of American Church in Berlin, Germany.

Professor, Columbia Theological Seminary, Decatur, Ga., 1928-30.

President, Queens College, Charlotte, N. C., 1939-1950.

Vice-chairman, Commission on Christian Education of National Council of Churches of Christ, 1950—.

Author of four books and numerous articles, reviews, etc.

# A Time for Decision

## PRESBYTERIANS LOOK TO THE FUTURE

## *Hunter B. Blakely*

### Presbyterians Look to the Future

IT IS time now for Presbyterians to make a momentous decision: Are we seriously in this business of Christian higher education? Is Christian higher education going to be big and important business? Whoever captures the campuses of today will control the culture and the civilization of tomorrow.

Recently an educator sat at lunch with four executives who had their fingers as sensitively placed on American business as any men in this country. The educator repeated to the group what has been said often the last few years: "Business and industry, the Federal Government in its program for the armed services and top administrative positions, are not asking education today for technical training for the job so much as for the preparation of the minds of men to think, to evaluate data, to take information and draw from the facts correct conclusions." Then he finished with the question: "Would you gentlemen, who so intimately know American business, agree that the primary need today is not for technical training but for that broader education in which the student learns how to use the tools of thought?"

"You are wrong," answered the spokesman of the four business executives.

Somewhat nonplussed by the emphatic answer, the educator inquired, "If what business needs most is not the preparation of

161

the intellect for logical thinking, what *is* the first demand on education?"

With emphasis the reply came: "The building of *character* is the greatest need. What I am looking for all the time in my business, and what every business man of my acquaintance seeks, are men and women of character and integrity—young people to whom I can entrust responsibility with the knowledge that they will do their best. The abilities for intellectual, logical thinking are important, but far more urgent is moral integrity."

The other business leaders nodded in agreement.

Our country today needs more than big machines run by little men. The campuses of America constitute the greatest evangelistic opportunity with which the Church has been confronted. It is the concern of the Church that moral and spiritual values be instilled in all education. Unless the Church seriously supports and guides Christian higher education, who can be expected to do this work for God?

The Methodist Church believes that Christian influence in education is important and has organized its personnel and resources for activity on American campuses. With an outburst of enthusiasm the Southern Baptist Church has gotten behind its colleges and seminaries, with the result that today no group of institutions is making greater progress. The Lutheran Church, in all its branches, is committed to an aggressive program of Christian higher education. With that long-range vision so characteristic of its history, the Roman Catholic Church is establishing new colleges all across America, strengthening old institutions, and on all major campuses is conducting well-organized programs for religious work.

The real war of our day is a battle of ideas, a competing for the minds of the educated leaders of tomorrow. Wherever the Communists can, in other parts of the world, they seek to control the colleges and universities. Thank God, little Communist influence now exists in American universities and colleges, for our faculties and administrators are among America's most loyal and patriotic citizens.

Recently there was completed under a grant from the Rockefeller and Carnegie Foundations perhaps the most comprehensive and exhaustive study of American higher education ever made in this country. In the volume, *The Development and Scope of Higher Education in the United States*, the first sentence reads: "There are several major themes that command the attention of the historian of American higher education, but among these the oldest and the longest sustained is the drift toward secularism."[1] Is the Church concerned about that drift away from spiritual and moral values? Can a great civilization continue to exist upon an increasingly secularist foundation?

## It Is Time for Decision—Now

If the Presbyterian Church in the United States is to have an important role in capturing the campuses for Christ, it must act now.

Higher education in America is on the march. Never before in the history of mankind has a nation attempted to make higher education so nearly universal. If, as some believe, 50 per cent of the American young people will continue their educations beyond high school by 1970, the colleges of America must then care for 6⅔ million students, almost 2½ times the present enrollment. We are spending today for higher education $50 for every dollar spent in 1900. It is difficult to estimate what American higher education will cost in 1970.

What results will come to our nation from this vast increase in college graduates? Will we have more training without corresponding character? Will we have more people befuddled and lost because they have found a bigger universe and have not discovered any points of permanent reference from which they can take bearings and chart a course for meaningful living?

Before 1900, few foreign students came to the United States. This year in American colleges and universities more than 40,000 students will be enrolled from other countries. To an ever increasing degree, the prosperity and the progress of America are based upon our system of higher education, and our world influence is linked closely with our schools.

At top levels the Federal Government and the states are carefully evaluating higher education programs and making plans. The great corporations and foundations are concerned about the future of American colleges and universities. Many studies of various kinds are in progress. From these the future of American higher education will be charted.

Wise decisions about the future of Presbyterian higher education will demand careful thinking and planning from our able leaders, both laymen and ministers. Rising and inflationary costs have placed a crippling burden on our colleges and seminaries. If we continue to drift rather than face this fact realistically, the tide will carry us beyond the point of no recall, and we shall discover that our schools have degenerated into second-rate institutions.

Within our Presbyterian colleges, both trustees and faculties must rise to creative thinking and planning, throwing off nostalgia and recognizing that today will never become yesterday and tomorrow will always lie beyond today.

The strategic planning by Presbyterians for the future must be governed not by emotions but by good common business judgment. If we need a new college in a certain area of our Church, we should plan to have it. If in another area we have too many weak schools, then old emotional loyalties should not keep Presbyterians from developing instead one strong, useful, reorganized institution. In this dynamically changing age there is no valid reason to maintain the status quo just because it is traditional.

## People of a Heritage

Presbyterians are people of a great heritage. It was the conviction of our ancestors that piety and intelligence must ever walk together. They believed that faith gave power but knowledge gave direction. They linked closely together in their planning the church and the schoolhouse.*

It was largely through emphasis on and consecration to education that Presbyterians had great influence. Their educated men and women became leaders for the young and growing nation. It

---

* See Chapters 2 and 3.

is true that in those days Presbyterians lagged behind in evangelism and missionary outreach and hence failed to become numerically one of America's largest denominations. Seemingly God was using a variety of builders for this new world civilization. While some religious groups were penetrating with the pioneers into forest and wilderness to keep America Christian, others were consolidating the position for a Christian America back along the territories which were being claimed for civilization. The great contribution of men of the Reformed faith to America's culture was that they were the molders of opinion. They were the educational leaders who did much to fashion the form of government, the social structure, the very thinking of early America.

Shall we Presbyterians of the twentieth century forfeit our heritage of being molders of American culture? Probably we can never recoup our lost opportunity of being numerically the largest denomination in America. The question is whether we are willing to surrender the privilege of being one of the most influential groups in fashioning the culture of the twenty-first century, now in process of creation. The America of tomorrow needs to have embedded into its thinking those vigorous Presbyterian convictions—the Sovereignty of God, the responsibility of every individual to God's holy will, the Lordship of Jesus Christ above every earthly loyalty, and the stamina of moral convictions which comes from such sturdy faith. Our fathers made their impact upon the nation through their ability to think creatively as Christians. Only a people vitally concerned to be both religious and intelligent can ever hope to shape the culture of their day as did the American Presbyterians of the eighteenth and nineteenth centuries.

## The Dynamically Developing Southland

The Presbyterian Church in the United States has its work located in the fast-growing South. After a century of struggle, the South is at last developing beyond anything that could have been imagined. Industries from other sections are moving into our part of the nation; new factories are springing up all across the South;

the whole economic and social structure is undergoing rapid and significant change. It is a new day of opportunity.

It is tremendously important that Presbyterians do their part to capture the campuses for Christ in this new South. No part of our nation needs more educated leaders for business and industry, for school and church, than does the South. Yet the percentage of youth attending college falls to a lower average in the Southern states. We in this period of opportunity cannot afford the loss of potential leadership. We must be concerned that able Southern youth get a good education while at the same time retaining Christian faith.

Our homes call for Presbyterians to advance in their program of Christian higher education. The American home is threatened by divorce, a rising crime rate, juvenile delinquency, parental delinquency, and the loss of a true sense of values. The home needs educated Christians with wisdom, imagination, and vision to restore the Christian's sense of values and to work out adjustments for Christian homemaking.

Over the next two years the nation's capacity for education must be increased in elementary schools by 25 per cent, in high schools by 75 per cent, in colleges by 50 per cent. Where will the teachers come from? Will the teachers of tomorrow be Christians? The last is perhaps the more important question.

Our Church, if it is to go forward, must immediately move toward these Forward with Christ objectives of 1955-57:

1. More consecrated laymen and women to undergird the work of our Church by prayer, work, and gifts.

2. More ministers to serve 312 new churches, to be pastors for 150,000 new members, to guide 150,000 new Sunday school pupils, and to man more than 550[2] vacant churches. In 1954 our Church had approximately 1,000 candidates for the ministry; in 1957 our Church hopes to have 1,600 candidates for the ministry.

3. More church workers with professional training. In 1954 there was a shortage of all kinds of full-time church workers, particularly directors of Christian education.

4. More missionaries to carry the Gospel of our Saviour to the world.

A denomination with such a program for a three-year period will have even greater manpower needs when these objectives are reached. Growth now will mean greater growth in the decades that follow.

Our world calls for the products of Christian higher education. In all human history, educated Christian men and women were never more needed. Our world needs statesmen, diplomats, business representatives abroad, educators for foreign appointments, missionaries, scientists, economists, writers, composers, and artists.

What answer will Presbyterians give to the calls upon Christian higher education?

## Presbyterians on the Job

It is time for all Presbyterians to be actively concerned about preparing our educated leadership of tomorrow.

In the home and in the local church we can begin by interpreting to youth the Christian view of lifework. Through the new program of Christian vocational guidance, described in Chapter 8 of this book, the Church has opportunities to help young people in an area which concerns them all.

When the Church shows its eagerness to do something for them that they believe is very important to their future, young people are drawn closer into its fellowship. We can claim youth in new enthusiasm and loyalty as they see that every Christian may be a full-time worker for Christ. It is in this program of vocational guidance that every parent, church school teacher, church officer, and minister can take hold of the job of preparing youth for tomorrow.

Our Campus Christian Life Department must be strengthened and assisted all along the line, from local congregations on through synods to the General Assembly level. This department is interested in over 50,000 students and over 5,000 Presbyterian faculty members.

Our Westminster Fellowships on Presbyterian, state, and independent campuses are the arms of the Church reaching out into 173 universities and colleges to prepare students for dedicated Christian living.

Our Presbyterian Faculty Fellowship, with its vision of enlisting in Christ's cause the more than 5,000 Presbyterian faculty members in Southern institutions, deserves the Church's prayers and interest.

---

THE FACTS ARE THESE:

- In 1900, two of every ten youths attended high schools.

- In 1954, eight of every ten youths attended high schools.

\* \* \*

- In 1900, two of every 100 young people went to college.

- In 1954, twenty of every 100 young people went to college.

\* \* \*

- About 2,200,000 young people are 18 years of age.

- Of these, about 550,000 are capable of good college work.

- But only 220,000 of the best qualified boys and girls will go to college. Only 118,000 will be graduated. The percentage of qualified youth going to college in the South is below the national average. Yet the South, with its expanding economy, needs college-trained leaders more than do most other sections.

- The nation's schools desperately need well-prepared Christian teachers. Enrollments in elementary schools have increased 24 per cent and in high schools 10 per cent, while the output of elementary and high school teachers has dropped 20 per cent since 1950.

---

We have our Presbyterian colleges—twenty-three of them. It is expensive business to maintain colleges. It will cost even more in the future. The salary increases in church colleges are lagging far behind the raises already made in tax-supported institutions. It is increasingly difficult to obtain good teachers. Much of the equipment in church colleges has become obsolete. The buildings frequently show the ravages of time. Administrators grow old prematurely as they struggle to balance budgets. College presidents are often lonely men, who know that they have been entrusted with important work and then left with the job on their hands and few to help.

Presbyterians cannot afford to withdraw from the field of higher education. Here are real and vital reasons why the Church must maintain colleges and improve them.

1. The church colleges must send a sufficient number of graduates into the educational stream to influence both its direction and its content. Without the church colleges American education would be poorer, and in turn the Church would lose much of its power to influence the culture of our country. As members of one denomination we do not do this alone. We Presbyterians join forces with those of other denominations. When we keep our colleges strong and vigorous we are taking part in the great work of some 700 church-related institutions of higher education. This active church connection makes an impact for Christian faith upon all of American education from the kindergarten to the postgraduate community.

2. The strength of American higher education is largely the result of its freedom from restrictive control. Unlike educators of the old world, our forefathers carefully planned that education in this new land should remain free. They established a dual system of higher education, in which up until 1947 the majority of American college students were in private and church colleges and universities. Recently the shift has been to a majority in state tax-supported institutions. Presbyterians led in establishing this dual system, and we, too, must make every possible effort and sacrifice to keep our institutions of higher learning strong as safeguards for human freedom.

3. It is still the church college which prepares approximately 70 per cent of the ministers and missionaries of the Church. Without our colleges and seminaries we would lack consecrated leadership, both lay and ministerial, for tomorrow's Church.

4. It is the Church's task to put the imprint of quality upon education. The only kind of church college education which is worthy of the name is quality education—intellectually, morally, spiritually.

5. It is obvious to every thoughtful Presbyterian that our

schools of theology and our school for preparing professional lay workers for the Church must be kept strong and provided with resources to keep up with a growing Church.

Too many of our colleges were established on "shoestring" resources. If we start a new college it must not open its doors until we can be sure it will not limp along with inadequate resources, uncertain of its future. Any new college should be established so firmly that immediately it will occupy a place of prestige and leadership.

Our larger task is with the institutions which we now have. They must be strengthened for their greatest opportunities. Within each college the trustees, administration, and faculty should plan carefully, intelligently, and purposefully to have a first-rate educational institution that is authentically Christian.

Each controlling synod has a responsibility to see that such planning is done. Through proper committees the synod should participate in the planning and help provide the means by which the goals of Christian service in education may be reached.

Some of our colleges are now operating with student bodies too small for efficiency, both educationally and financially. Frequently there is inadequate dormitory space. Our colleges should be large enough to be efficient educational units, but small enough to maintain that close personal relationship of faculty with student so essential to the best in Christian education.

It should be the concern of every Presbyterian to know more about the colleges of our Church and to direct young people to a consideration of a Presbyterian college as they plan for their education.

Presbyterians need to turn concern into action—the kind of action that costs in giving, in making bequests, and most of all in active planning, praying, and working to make our Presbyterian institutions worthy of our Church and her future.

Colleges and seminaries are not built in a day. The campuses of America must be recaptured afresh in every student generation. Good Christian education is never a mushroom, overnight product. It is a growth of decades of patient, far-seeing planning, hard work, and consecration.

## With Eyes to the Future

Our world is not finished. It, in fact, has just begun. John Steinbeck has unusual ability to put his finger on a sore spot in American life. In his little book, *The Red Pony*, is a story of the conquest of this continent by the pioneers, ever westering across rivers, prairies, deserts, mountains, and then finally down to the ocean. The final pages present an old grandfather telling his grandson, Jody, of the adventurous trek and how grandfather had been a leader in that adventure. The old man finished:

"Then we came down to the sea, and it was done." He stopped and wiped his eyes . . .

"Maybe I could lead the people some day," Jody said.

The old man smiled. "There's no place to go. There's the ocean to stop you. There's a line of old men along the shore hating the ocean because it stopped them."

"In boats I might, sir."

"No place to go, Jody. Every place is taken. But that's not the worst—no, not the worst. Westering has died out of the people. Westering isn't a hunger any more. It's all done. Your father is right. It is finished."[3]

"Westering," the spirit of adventure, must not die in the hearts of American people. Our country is the result of the toil of adventurers. The Christian faith is a call to adventure.

Adventures of the future will largely be in the areas of the mind—new discoveries, new machines, new forces to be unleashed, new remedies for human disease, new plans for political, economic, and social life.

It is time for Presbyterians to do strategic planning in education. We of course must conserve the worth-while work which we now have, strengthening it all along the line. But we also need to be creative and imaginative about other areas of education which may be important in the days ahead. What should be done by the Church in that rapidly expanding program of adult education? Education has an opportunity to help individuals become more proficient in their own vocations and at the same time learn how to relate daily work more meaningfully to Christian faith. It is possible that members of the Reformed family of churches are missing an opportunity to influence culture because they have no school to send out leaders trained in such areas as international relations, government, sociology, and education. Has it not been the genius of men of the Reformed faith that their religion enabled them to be pioneers of progress?

Today we have the world that is; as Christians we dream and plan and work for the world as God would have it. Said Plato, "You cannot improve the world unless you improve men. . . . Governments reflect human nature. States are not made out of stone or wood, but out of the character of their citizens; these turn the scale and draw everything after them." Plato was correct: we will never get a beautiful and peaceful world until we get beautiful and peaceable people to live in it.

Jesus Christ contributed that which Plato had left out. He showed that God by salvation made new men, changed human hearts, gave purposeful motivation, set believers at tasks in accordance with God's purposes. By the power of the great redemption, God made men right with God, with their neighbors, and with themselves. Then by educating men He quickened their abilities, directed their activities, and set them at worth-while tasks.

Our planet's future will depend not so much on the discovery of new methods, the building of bigger machines, the releasing of new material resources in the earth or sea or sky. The future depends most on discovering and releasing for Christian purposes and under spiritual control those vast possibilities which are in the personalities of the boys and girls of today, who tomorrow will handle our destinies.

# What the
# Local Church Can Do

In 1956, designated by the General Assembly as a year of emphasis on higher education, local Presbyterian churches can take highly important steps of long-range influence.

*1. Complete organization under the church Committee on Christian Education which will permit a continuing program on higher education. Normally, this would be through a sub-committee.*

2. *Develop the Presbyterian Guidance Program for youth of your church.*

   a. Provide pre-vocational guidance for high school and older youth.

   b. Refer youth to Presbyterian Guidance Centers, usually found in a Presbyterian college within one day's driving distance.

   c. Find or provide financial aid for students going to college.

   d. Assist your young people in starting lifework and homes.

3. *Follow your young people to college.*

   a. Introduce your boys and girls to pastors of churches at their colleges, by letter or in person.

   b. Send them your church bulletins.

   c. Send your church paper, carrying news of students.

   d. Use students in church program when they return for holidays.

   e. Inform students of special study and work opportunities—seminars, work camps, conferences, etc.

f. Help students find summer occupations for vocational exploration and to help finance their college careers.

4. *Foster contacts with synod and Church institutions.*

   a. Arrange visits to campuses.
   b. Invite speakers, choir, etc., from our colleges.
   c. Promote visits to colleges by young people of your church.
   d. Sponsor worthy students at college.
   e. Post and distribute church college literature.
   f. Encourage young people to consider attending church colleges.

5. *Participate fully in financial campaigns for higher education when directed by your synod.*

6. *Participate in Year of Emphasis on Higher Education.*

   a. Encourage reading of the book on Higher Education, *Church and Campus*, obtainable from Presbyterian Book Stores.
   b. Order special literature from Division of Higher Education, Box 1176, Richmond, Virginia.
   c. Women of the Church and Men of the Church: Use the book, *Church and Campus*; have panel discussion on Higher Education; promote trips to our church colleges, seminaries, and Training School; invite speakers from colleges and universities; support synod objectives for higher education; co-operate in setting up Presbyterian Guidance Program in local church.
   d. Young people: Have panel discussion on Westminster Fellowship; invite students from our nearby institutions; visit our colleges; participate in Presbyterian Guidance Program.
   e. Pastor: Encourage full participation in Presbyterian Guidance Program. Inform church of our program in higher education.
   f. Director of Christian Education: Make sure that local church program includes specific plans for higher education interests—especially in work with young people. Secure *Church and Campus* for church library.
   g. Plan Family Night programs in which Christian higher education is main topic.
   h. Work toward an informed Church which will give our educational institutions its prayers and support.

# Acknowledgments

**CHAPTER 1**

THE CRITICAL YEARS *by J. J. Murray*

1. Sir Walter Moberly, *The Crisis in the University*, p. 73. London: SCM Press, Ltd., 1949. Used by permission of The Macmillan Company.
2. Elton Trueblood, quoted in the religious press. Used by permission of the author.

**CHAPTER 2**

FOR DIGNITY OF MAN AND GLORY OF GOD *by Francis Pickens Miller*

1. John Calvin, *Institutes*, IV, XX, 32.
2. John Witherspoon, sermon delivered at Princeton, N. J., on May 17, 1776, extracts from which are published in a brochure by Stewart M. Robinson entitled "The Political Thought of the Colonial Clergy" (privately printed).

**CHAPTER 3**

BLOOD, SWEAT, AND PRAYERS *by R. T. L. Liston*

1. *Works of Rufus Choate*, Vol. I, p. 378. Little, Brown and Co., 1862.
2. From the Witherspoon Monument, Washington, D. C.
3. In *The Iron Worker*, Vol. XVIII, No. 1, Winter 1953-54, p. 5. Published by the Lynchburg Foundry Co., Lynchburg, Va.
4. Hugh Blair Grigsby, in a Centennial address in 1876, reminiscing of the College as he had known it in 1815. *The Iron Worker, op. cit.*, p. 5.
5. Allen E. Ragan, *History of Tusculum College*, pp. 37-38.
6. Edwin E. Slosson, *The American Spirit in Education*, p. 62.
7. *Ibid.*, p. 60.
8. *Ibid.*

9. Anonymous, *U. S. Census 1860: Mortality and Miscellaneous Statistics*, p. 505.
10. William Stuart Red, *A History of the Presbyterian Church in Texas*, p. 251. Copyright 1936 by the Steck Company.
11. *The Iron Worker, op. cit.*, p. 9.
12. *Ibid.*
13. *A Study of Stillman Institute*, pp. 49-50. Edited by Paul W. Terry and L. Tennent Lee. University of Alabama Press, 1946.
14. F. D. Jones and W. H. Mills, *The Presbyterian Church in South Carolina Since 1850*. Copyright 1926 by the Synod of South Carolina, Columbia, S. C.

## CHAPTER 4

## WHAT IS A CHRISTIAN COLLEGE? *by John R. Cunningham*

1. Gordon Gray, in the Charter Day address delivered at the University of California in Los Angeles on March 25, 1955. Used by permission.
2. William Allen White. Quoted in *The Educational Institutions Survey*, Synod of North Carolina, 1955.
3. William M. Compton, in Commencement address at Davidson College, 1955.
4. From *The Educational Institutions Survey, op. cit.*
5. From leaflet, "Why Choose a Church College," by Samuel R. Spencer, Jr. Division of Higher Education, Board of Christian Education, Presbyterian Church, U. S.
6. Zechariah 4:6.

## CHAPTER 5

## THE PRESBYTERIAN MARK: AN EDUCATED LEADERSHIP
*by E. T. Thompson*

1. William Maxwell, *A Memoir of the Rev. John H. Rice*, pp. 232-233. Published by J. Whetham, Philadelphia, 1835.
2. Manuscript Records, Presbyterian Foundation, Montreat, N. C.
3. Louis C. LaMotte, *Colored Light—The Story of the Influence of Columbia Seminary 1828-1936*, p. 40. Published for the author by Presbyterian Committee of Publication, Richmond, Va. Copyright 1937 by Louis C. LaMotte, Clinton, S. C.
4. L. W. Bacon, *A History of American Christianity*, p. 292. Charles Scribner's Sons, 1923. By permission of the publishers.
5. R. S. Sanders, *History of Louisville Presbyterian Theological Seminary*, p. 34. Published by Louisville Theological Seminary, Louisville, Ky.
6. *Ibid.*, p. 45.

7. William Stuart Red, *A History of the Presbyterian Church in Texas*, pp. 308-309. The Steck Company.
8. Sanders, *op. cit.*, p. 96.
9. From a brochure, "A Great Door Is Opened," published by Union Theological Seminary in Virginia, 1952.
10. Minutes of the General Assembly, 1930, pp. 120-121.
11. From *Life*, October 31, 1949. Quoted with permission of the publishers in *The Changing South* by E. T. Thompson, p. 112, John Knox Press.

## CHAPTER 6

## CAMPUS CHRISTIAN LIFE *by Malcolm C. McIver*

1. Definition given by the *Archbishops' Committee of Inquiry on the Evangelistic Work of the Church*. Quoted in *Towards the Conversion of England*, p. 1. The Press and Publications Board of the Church Assembly, Westminster, 1945.
2. Sir Walter Moberly, *The Crisis in the University*, p. 57. London: SCM Press, Ltd., 1949.
3. Students selected the name Westminster Fellowship to emphasize the importance of the beliefs of the Presbyterian Church found in our Westminster *Confession of Faith*.
4. *Campus Christian Life Manual*, p. 31. Board of Christian Education, Richmond, Virginia, 1953.
5. Quoted from an unpublished letter.
6. *Campus Christian Life Manual, op. cit.*, p. 37.
7. *Principles, Policies, and Procedures*, p. 27. Board of Christian Education, Presbyterian Church, U.S.A., Philadelphia, 1954.
8. *Ibid.*, p. 17.
9. *Ibid.*, p. 27.
10. *Campus Christian Life Manual, op. cit.*, p. 7.
11. *Ibid.*
12. *Ibid.*

## CHAPTER 9

## A TIME FOR DECISION *by Hunter B. Blakely*

1. Richard Hofstadter and C. DeWitt Hardy, *The Development and Scope of Higher Education in the United States*, p. 3. Columbia University Press, 1952. Used by permission.
2. Figure for 1954.
3. John Steinbeck, *The Red Pony*, pp. 129-130. Copyright 1937-1938 by John Steinbeck. Used by permission of The Viking Press, Inc., publishers.